Nagged, Tagged and Bagged . . .

Divorce Recovery

Victoria

I hope you enjoy

By Keith G Churchouse

© *April 2011*

SIGN HERE,
HERE AND HERE!...

JOURNEY OF A FINANCIAL ADVISER

Keith Churchouse

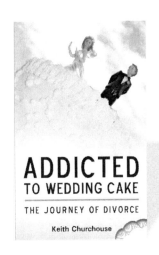

ADDICTED
TO WEDDING CAKE

THE JOURNEY OF DIVORCE

Keith Churchouse

The Churchouse Chronicles©

The first in the series of Churchouse Chronicles is the book,

Sign here, here and here! . . . Journey of a Financial Adviser

www.signherehereandhere.co.uk

Released March 2010

Available in paperback and e-reader ISBN: 978-0-9564325-0-6

Reviews:

'...useful information imparted in a humorous and courageous manner by a long serving and successful advocate for a new professional approach'.
S.Williams

'I found that the book clearly shows the reader how to operate with humour, confidence and above all honesty'.
M.Drakeford

The second in the series of Churchouse Chronicles is the book,

Journey of Divorce, Addicted to Wedding Cake

www.addictedtoweddingcake.co.uk

Released June 2010

Available in paperback and e-reader ISBN: 978-0-9564325-2-0

Reviews:

'..you can flip to the section that you need advice on or read through it and get a handle on each stage of the process. I have already recommended it to several friends who are divorcing because I really think it will help them.'
L. Busnell-Lane

His writing style is easy, informative and light. With just the right amount of humour which never debases, nor makes fun, he creates an atmosphere of understanding. Congratulations!
J.Walker

ISBN 978-0-9564325-4-4

Further contact details and information can be found at www.naggedtaggedandbagged.co.uk

No financial advice of any description is offered or deemed to have been provided during the text of this book.

No legal advice of any description is offered or deemed to have been provided during the text of this book.

Some of the names, titles, sequencing, areas and dates in this book have been amended to ensure that this work portrays a personal experience rather than those of individuals or companies. Any similarity is purely coincidental.

This book is also an expression of the personal opinion of the author.

A donation will be made to the charity *Association for Spina Bifida and Hydrocephalus for each book sold.* Registered Charity No: 249338. *www.asbah.org*

Acknowledgements

Esther Dadswell

The first acknowledgement and thanks has to go to Esther, my wife, who has provided help and experience in the process of collating this text. I have often joked that I have become your ghost writer and I thank you for the privilege of your input and wise words.
I could not have taken the best part of my own divorce recovery and journey without you.

Love always.

My parents, Rosamund and Roger Churchouse

Thank you for also putting up with me even though I am remarried!
Thank you for standing by me to mop up the pieces and supporting Esther on my journey of recovery.
Thank you also for allowing me time to find myself and guiding me on how to start again.

You were right: there is life after divorce, although I did not see it so clearly at the time. And the journey has been exciting to say the least!

To my survey respondents

Thank you for spending your time and wisdom in helping with your own experiences of divorce recovery. Your input has been most valuable and you know who you are.

To the guiding hands that have helped me with this book

Thanks to:

*Graham Booth, Creation Booth,
contact: www.creationbooth.com*

*Fiona Cowan, Words That Work,
contact: fifix@btopenworld.com*

*Jo Parfitt, Creative Mentor,
contact: www.joparfitt.com*

*Tom Evans, The Bookwright,
contact: www.thebookwright.com*

To my learned friend, Kim Finnis

*Thank you to Kim Finnis, a divorce lawyer of the
highest calibre based in Guildford, who has cast her
learned eyes over the text. Thank you for all of your
help, support and consideration. Kim's foreword
follows in the next section.*

Accompanying Website

www.naggedtaggedandbagged.co.uk

Contents

Forewords..10

    Esther Dadswell..10

    Kim Finnis...13

Introduction..15

Got the T-shirt 23

Looking back..39

Signposts 63

Stress 83

Health and wellbeing...95

The process of change...115

Money matters 131

Being comfortable on your own.........................159

Church, House and Mr Lightyear.................177

Opportunity knocks..199

Resources 214

Useful Websites...217

About the author...221

Forewords

Esther Dadswell

It was my own decision to leave my ex-husband, but that didn't make it any easier. Nor did it stop me from questioning my choices or prevent the tears and guilt over my perceived selfishness.

I'd lived a charmed childhood, with a wealth of experiences some of which, even now, I still have to pinch myself to believe. At 18, I had drawn up a wish list of all the things I wanted to do, and completed it by age 35. My list included marriage, children, suburbia, the Porsche on the drive, a degree ….you understand the sort of list. I married a good man and had a lovely daughter, but my life was not complete. Something was missing.

As time went on, the feeling of the 'missing part' in my life became more apparent and my desire to make changes grew.

As I discovered later, the element missing from my life was *excitement*. I needed to *do something every day that scared me*. I needed a feeling of freedom. I know that many of you won't understand how I have freedom now, living and working with my current husband, but I do. I make decisions and choices every day that affect our lives together. I still daydream of going to the Galapagos or Easter Islands, or climbing to Base Camp on Everest.

These are things we will achieve together, and with the last of these goals, maybe raise some more funds for the charity, ASBHA.

In the course of my personal development, I have learnt to scuba dive and have a licence to drive a powerboat; things I don't think I would have achieved in my first marriage. It wasn't until I did my first 'try dive' that I found peace, under the water with no phones, no emails, no nagging or screaming, and only the Picasso Triggerfish to contend with. For that sense of peace, I adore diving and try to go whenever the water is clear and warm.

Divorce is hard work and recovery can be even harder. Restoring self-dignity was always going to be an interesting trip. It was my choice to leave, but this did not stop me feeling crap about the decision. As you will see from some of the responses to Keith's survey, later in this book, I am not alone in having those feelings. In the same survey, you'll also see I am also not alone in seeing the beneficial outcome of making changes in life.

Although married to Keith, I haven't taken his surname. This does upset a few family members, especially when I have to return their mis-named cheques at Christmas time, but it still gives me the feeling of independence. I didn't want to change my name when I married the first time, but it was expected. I joke this time that it's to keep the costs down, especially with Keith's somewhat dubious track record for marriage, but deep down I know it's my independent streak showing through.

I feel that I have grown both in myself and in my relationship. This has expanded my horizons, a white-knuckle ride at times. There have been some dark moments, misunderstandings and much laughter. Looking back at what has been accomplished, would I take the ride again? There is only one answer and it is a big 'YES!'

Esther Dadswell is a director of Churchouse Financial Planning Limited and is married to Keith Churchouse.

Kim Finnis

Divorce involves a fundamental life change. For most people it is a time of considerable stress and emotional turmoil, along with anxiety as to what the future may hold.

In *Nagged, Tagged & Bagged* Keith explores the process of recovering from divorce, which he describes as a personal and unique journey of learning and understanding.

Nagged, Tagged and Bagged offers those who have been through divorce a thought provoking guide to creating a fulfilling future. It also contains practical tips with exercises and space for notes. The book takes a sensitive and informed approach to the various issues that have to be tackled on this journey. Keith's easy to read style and sharing of his personal experiences definitely makes this an essential book for those intent on re-building their lives after divorce.

Kim Finnis,
Family Lawyer, Collaborative Lawyer and Mediator
Kim Finnis, Solicitor, Guildford, Surrey
www.kimfinnis.co.uk

Nagged, Tagged and Bagged...

Introduction

It's not your fault you are divorced. Or is it? Were the chasms that opened up between you and your ex-spouse just programmed into your DNA? Now that the nagging of the past union has stopped, you have, possibly willingly, picked up the tag of *divorcee*, bagged up your belongings and are now alone. Does it really matter whose fault it was?

In this modern world, you may have both led separate lives and just shared the same bed, passing like ships in the night. It was only when the focus of a fortnight's summer holiday or ten days' 'family time' over Christmas came about that the metaphorical straw broke the camel's back and your marriage folded.

Are you a person of the past, crying over spilt milk, or are you a person of the future, looking forward to the new reinvigorated reinvented you?

I am sure that the Court documentation may state who divorced whom and what marital crimes were committed to allow the divorce petition to occur in the first place. I have little doubt you will remember those dark days. But the reality is that rarely can any one party to a marriage that hits the rocks say that they had nothing to do with their relationship's demise. If an individual does say that, it's possible that their arrogance if not ignorance was the cause.

The most difficult time in the separation might have been the 'bagging' sessions of moving out, which to some extent is the only physical part of the divorce process. Aside from a flurry of legal paperwork and a dent in your bank account, the boxing and bagging of your personal belongings can be emotional. It is likely to involve moving you or your ex-spouse out or selling the family home.

The final disagreements about who owns what and the possibility of being moved out without notice or much communication might be resolved by your ex-spouse *helpfully* putting all of what he or she considers to be 'your' things in storage — without being at all biased about selecting those items — and then telling you where you can collect them from. It has the potential to make you feel maudlin or fraught, leaving you with emotional voids that were once filled with love and companionship. Anyone going through the divorce process needs to be ready for this.

I hope that now, having been through the full separation and the legal mangle of your divorce days, you have taken the positive step of reading this book in order to move on to the new life that is yours to explore. And move on you must. Remember, there are 240,000 or so other divorcing souls each year, and you are all in similar boats.

Life is too short to waste any more of it dwelling on the divorce process. Instead, it's time to reach towards the opportunities that only you desire.

Having been divorced twice and married three times, you may have figured out that I am happily married again and that, with my wife Esther, we have rebuilt our lives and flourished since our last foray into the divorce courts. Esther has offered me much support in preparing this book, along with a few other important individuals in my life. I often feel like her 'ghost writer'. However, you will see in this book her balancing influence, as you start to plan your own recovery from divorce. I have acknowledged her thoughts many times in this text. Again, I offer her my love and gratitude for her words of wisdom and experience as we have spent time recovering, restoring and building our futures together.

This gesture of thanks also points to the fact that this is to some extent a self help/self development/self motivational book. My concern with these types of book is that some people, mainly men, will find the idea of reading one a non-starter. For you, recovery may still seem an intangible goal — but you still need to deliver your objectives for your new future. This will mean change, action and energy from you. This text sets out to offer a practical path for your recovery, pulling no punches.

Most of us are not people of the past; we are naturally forward-looking. Esther is certainly one of these people, being one of the best forward thinkers I know, and I also count myself as another. (Esther might disagree with my judgement here, when she views my preference for late 70's and 80's music.) Forward thinking is one of the main drivers to success in my opinion.

You may have to dust yourself down after the finalisation of your divorce. Once that job is done, the way is clear for your new beginning.

Life is not a drill. Your recovery is not a dress rehearsal. Your life and your future begin here and I hope you are excited, if not inspired, by the prospect. I am sure that your personal optimism about the future may not be overwhelming at the start of your divorce recovery, given the settlement you received; it is up to you to overcome your feelings about that. There are no short cuts when it comes to divorce recovery.

Moving on and recovering, even blossoming, will take time, effort and money. In my first book, *Sign Here, Here and Here!* I referred to points in life when you come to a junction, or *'Life Junction'* as I call them. You sit at a crossroads and have to decide whether to go left, right or straight ahead. You may not have chosen to be at the crossroads — the separation and divorce may have put you there unexpectedly. Each possible route would take you in a completely different direction. Like driving any vehicle, sitting at the junction for the rest of your life is not an option. So, which way to go?

Each road will take you outside your comfort zone and that might be why you hesitate. Someone behind you could be blasting their horn to get you out of his or her way. A decision has to be made and quickly. Going outside your comfort zone is always scary; you discover eccentricities you never knew were there. It's also exciting. You may have to travel some distance down a road to find it is the wrong way. Both satellite navigation gadgets and life in general can do that to you.

Do you recognise yourself in this picture? It is just another *'Life Junction'* with another set of options available to you. Going outside your comfort zone also reveals more about what you are comfortable with in yourself.

Together, we will look at these points — but I will need a commitment from you. Together, we will need desire, *your* desire to be exact, to reinvent 'planet you' in the universe in which you want to live. You could argue that these thoughts are all about self belief, and to some extent that is true. You have self belief already. Maybe it's just a matter of rediscovering where you lost it, if you ever did? Perhaps you managed to hang on to your own belief; in which case, so much the better. As the fictional comedy character Austin Powers might put it: *'You've lost your Mojo!'*

Do you remember being 'you' before you got married? That younger, beautiful, funny, athletic, intellectual, robust, hardworking, possibly slimmer, humble, quiet you? Whatever you were and, in reality, still are, you will always remember that wonderful person. It might have been a few decades ago and since then the overdraft may have gone north while the waistline headed south, but many of us were happy then, before we got caught up in relationships, children, houses, mortgages, school fees and everything else you care to add to the list of life's burdens.

We will not dwell in the past, although a selective look at what effect this had on your outlook and demeanour is usually worthwhile — even if only to steer you away from what does not suit you. We will rediscover some of the best bits of the old you, mixed in with your new enlightened wisdom, and the values that made you happy and comfortable with yourself all that time ago. Above all, this should provide you with positive energy.

Although staring into the unknown is daunting at first, the prospect of recovery should fill you with excitement as we piece together the way change is going to have a positive effect in making your world a brilliant place to be.

Nagged, Tagged and Bagged...

Chapter One

Got the T-shirt

Oh, how life can change. Just imagine . . .

'Your champagne, ma'am,' said George with a smile, quietly immaculate in his perfectly-tailored black suit, placing a slender highball glass on the gently vibrating polished table that his employer had faced towards the rear of her Lear jet.

She hardly moved in the embrace of her large, cream leather seat as she stared wistfully out of the compartment window, the warm sun shining against the last of the French Alps below.

'I have taken the liberty of ordering up your Rolls convertible from the house, ma'am. The weather at Nice airport is very agreeable today and the house and staff are expecting you. Traffic to Monaco is reasonably light and I have been advised that your favourite table for tonight is reserved for 8.30. Claudette has called to suggest that the scallops are very much at their best. Shall I have the Rolls ready or will you be driving yourself tonight, ma'am?'

'You can drive the Rolls tonight, thank you, George,' she replied, having now turned her attention to a story on the front of the folded pink *Financial Times* in front of her. She briefly looked up to acknowledge the incoming messages provided by George, before taking a gentle sip from her glass.

'Tomorrow, George, I would like to go out on the yacht — and please can you find me somewhere *nice* for lunch? You know what a *disaster* the place was last month! Tell John to head towards Italy this time. I have a nautical feel at the moment and we might carry on down the coast,' she ordered in a soft tone, a slight frown at the thought of that last lunch subsiding.

A muffled chirp came from her yellow Louis Vuitton bag and she reached down to the deep pile fawn carpet to retrieve her gold mobile phone as it accepted a text.

'Ah!' she beamed. 'It's Patrick. He will be joining us tomorrow. Excellent! We have a guest tomorrow, George, so please make sure that the household staff and John make the necessary preparations.' She was glowing with the thought that her latest trip along the Cote d'Azur had just become a little more interesting.

'Very good, ma'am,' came the prompt reply from George, nodding slightly to acknowledge the instructions.

'Oh! And George, what is that thumping noise coming from rear of the plane? It sounds terrible!' she growled, as she began to stir uncomfortably in her seat.

The thumping grew louder as she slowly and unwillingly drifted out of the depths of her dream and flickers from an orange streetlight streamed through the ill-fitting curtains. An unusual smile was welded to her face, an emotion she had not felt for some time, as her sleepy eyes stirred into focus. The leather clad Lear jet cabin was nowhere to be seen as the rain tapped against the small window of her one-bedroom flat. It was still night and she peered with an awkward squint through the dark to see that it was not her usual six o'clock alarm call. It was only two in the morning and the thumping noise was in fact next door's stereo booming while they 'entertained' whoever they had managed to lay their hands on at the local nightclub.

Remembering she had work in the morning, the sinking feeling of reality sank in and a tear trickled slowly down her cheek as she huddled under the duvet to keep the cold from reaching any further. The thumping noise soon matched the thump in her head from the effects of a mild headache as her weary eyes closed and she tried without success to retrieve her champagne and French Riviera dream. All too soon, the unwelcome alarm barked its morning call and real life dragged her from the partial sanctuary of her interrupted slumber.

The night, like her uncomfortable previous marriage, was over and the new day and beginning beckoned.

Have you ever noticed how dreams don't usually contain much Nagging, Tagging or Bagging? And if they do, you tend to wake up and end it. Sadly, in real life, you cannot shake off the nightmare of a recent divorce — but you can steer its outcome. Like bad dreams, you can choose to 'wake up' and change course. As you know, in the land of your dreams anything is possible.

None of us wants to dwell on the past, and in this book we are not going to. Together we will, however, reflect on its influences, learning points and experiences that will both stand you in good stead and strengthening your resolve. There is little point in raking over the coals of the dissolution of your marriage. As you know, we've all 'got the T-shirt' on that score and are already tired of having our parentage questioned by the previous incumbent.

The reality of the situation has probably been worse than any nightmare, especially with things divorce and separation related.

Or, I could be completely wrong about your circumstances. You may see your divorce as an early release from the debacle that was your marriage. Your new surroundings and bank balance may not be what they were before and I hope that you don't have a thumping stereo waking you up at night, having been demoted from your family home to a bedsit or alike.

However, I believe it would be remiss of me to start this journey or divorce recovery, looking forward to your brighter future, without at least drawing a line under where you have come from. To help with your recovery and looking to your future, there are fifteen exercises in total throughout the book to allow you to make a few important notes as you travel towards your divorce recovery. There are also notes pages at the end of each chapter to help collate your development thoughts. I anticipate that these will help with your forward planning

We do know that, to a greater or lesser extent, many of us have been 'nagged' before we divorced, 'tagged' with the divorce label and have moved on from our previous life, with our emotional and physical baggage in tow.

Have you ever stopped to think what those words really mean? Emotionally, they will mean different things to each of us and you may have different names for each word. I thought it might be useful to consider the definitions of each word from the title of this book, with help from the *Little Oxford Dictionary*. This may well place where you have come from in context:

Nagged (Nag)

Definition: Find fault (with) or scold persistently (at). Gnawing, persistent.

It might be unfair to say that these words sound familiar at the end of a marriage. For some people, a divorce can come like a bolt from the blue rather than having a sustained build-up and a period of dissatisfaction in the union. The waspish barbs of wisdom that once violated your thoughts may now be over because of the deterioration and end of your marriage. That might be because of marital infidelity or just a 'dear John' letter, saying that it's over; your ex-spouse may have bagged him – or herself up and have left without notice, citing some reason or other and confirming that they have had enough, that you never listened, or that they need to 'find themselves' — possibly in the arms of another party.

It is not a good idea to relive those closing days because often the wounds are still raw. However, if you are still at the beginning of your divorce, then I would recommend that you read my earlier book, *Journey of Divorce, Addicted to Wedding Cake*, to help you through the situation.

For those already at the 'Bagged' stage of the process, please have no concern about a positive outcome. We will be looking closely at the process and positives of recovery in the later chapters.

Tagged (Tag)

Definition: Label for tying on, brief and usually trite quotation, etc.

In looking up this definition, I was fascinated to see the word 'trite'. The definition for 'trite' is *well-worn, hackneyed, commonplace*. How apt is this definition in the context of divorce and picking up the label, or tag, of *divorcee*. With around 240,000 individuals going through a divorce each year in England and Wales (Source: National Statistics 2008) this shows that divorce is commonplace.

Add to this that the annual figure noted above is on the low side in comparison to other years, and you can see that holding the marital status of 'divorced' shows that you are not alone. With so many individuals getting divorced each year, it is unusual not to regularly meet those who already have the divorcee 'tag'.

Although I am not proud of the fact that I have two divorces to my record, I also feel strongly that it is not necessarily a negative tag or in itself a negative reflection on my character. Life does not stop after a divorce. How you move forward will determine the true outcome of the episode. And don't forget that it was just an episode. Like most television series, another episode will follow soon, with more drama to unfold.

As suggested on the back cover of this book, the late Henry Ford, founder of the Ford Motor Company, reportedly said that *'failure is simply the opportunity to start again, this time more intelligently'*. I was inspired when I recently heard this saying for the first time, because any failure teaches you something, even if you don't enjoy the lesson. We are all learning all the time, from cradle to grave. How you apply this new wisdom to your own personal circumstances will dictate whether you reach your target, objective or personal goal.

That raises the question of what that target or objective is. This is the first step on your divorce recovery. Whatever you choose, make it something *positive* to achieve. You need to think about this early in the process, because you're not going to get there if you don't know where you want to go — and indeed how you will know when you have completed your journey and reached your target.

You could say that this is the reinvention of you: the new wiser, happier, more content, sleeker you that will make you complete in the future.

Bagged (Bag)

Definition: Receptacle of flexible material with opening usually at the top. Put in bag, secure.

In the context of this book and all things divorce related, I think the last word, 'secure', is the real definition. Many people hope to secure their belongings after a divorce, although there are usually arguments over who owns which item and why. The truth is that most people would like to make a clean sweep of their old life and start afresh in a new one. You might want to think carefully before fighting for this or that item on a point of principle; as you found out with your marriage, when you finally got it you may realise that you did not want it after all.

Most importantly, you need to consider securing your future. Bringing along the clutter of your old life may slow that process down by providing too many reminders and memories of what has gone before. Inevitably, there will always be a few irreplaceable things, accumulated during the course of a marriage that will remain with you. But think about it from this point of view: was the decision to acquire 'X or Y' item in your marriage, your decision or a joint decision? If you had been on your own, would you now own that item? Even if the answer to this question is 'yes', taking into account your new circumstances and situation, do you still want it?

If the answer is 'no', then eBay.co.uk or any other auction website is only a few clicks away and I am sure you could put to better use the cash from a sale.

I know of one lady in our family whose husband died not long ago. His death was not entirely unexpected and after the funeral, some bagging and boxing of his things was undertaken and the boxes were safely stacked away. There were quite a lot of items to put away and a lockup was eventually employed to solve the immediate storage issue. Time has ticked by, and the issue of sorting out the contents of the boxes properly, and possibly getting rid of a few unwanted items, has stopped in its tracks. I believe that this is partly because her recovery from his loss has gone well and she does not want this interrupted. But she cherishes the memories of her late husband and these may be disturbed or disrupted by the act of going through the personal items that she may have forgotten. To do this now might open those freshly healed wounds and defeat the positive objectives.

Memories need to be treated with respect, because for some people this is all they ever wanted or all that is left.

The first three words, *Nagged, Tagged* and *Bagged* are the headlines of the title. You will note that they are all set in the past tense. They should now remain in the past tense for you, and I hope that the subtitle '*Divorce Recovery*' is the one that appealed when you parted with your cash to read the book.

Divorce recovery is a personal and unique *journey* of learning and understanding amongst other things, and the definitions of *Journey* and *Recovery* may help set the scene for our journey through the text of this book.

A definition of these two words are as follows:

Journey

Definition: Distance travelled; expedition to some distance, round of travel. Make journey.

Your recovery, like any other journey, is going to take time. You may just about know where you are, but may not know where you want to get to. We will consider together your personal targets for the future. These targets may need to be re-set for all aspects of your life: love, employment, your home, anything. Some people compare this thought to a hitchhike journey and all of the risks that this involves.

By the way, hitchhike, as illustrated by the lady on the front cover, has a definition of: *travel by means of lifts in vehicles.* Like a hitchhiker, you might know which general direction you want to go by selecting a road. What you don't know is which vehicle will stop to pick you up, who will be at the wheel and what their motivations were for pulling over to the side of the road. Having never hitch hiked myself, or pulled over to offer a lift, I cannot pretend to understand the physical experience. However, using this analogy for rebuilding a life after a divorce, then my rucksack and I have travelled far along roads that I never dreamed of, with people that I have never met before.

It can be daunting, however it broadens your experience and provides the potential for adventure. Lucky you, if you have this potential in prospect; many people don't and live to regret the missed opportunity.

Recovery

Definition: Regain possession or use or control of; reclaim; secure restitution (of) or compensation (for) by legal process; bring back to life, cease to feel effects of; retrieve.

I think this definition is excellent, and useful for defining the purpose of looking at your recovery in reclaiming, retrieving and bringing back to life your future.

Although this book focuses on recovery following a divorce or separation, recovery can also be applicable after other types of bereavement. I use the word *bereavement* because I do think that a period of reflection and grieving may be needed after a divorce to ensure that a secure foundation can be achieved to move your new life forward. It is like a period of saying goodbye to the old before being ready to welcome in the new. This may have its hurdles if your ex-spouse is collecting the children each agreed period, but this must not deter you from your goals.

It is up to you to decide how your future is going to look.

We are all different. The decision making process that has gone before may now have changed to a new style of self-focused arrangement; or, if you are with a new partner, a decision making process on your joint future. This will be the same for all your future decisions about what you wear, eat or drive, but also for where you live, your money, your work and even your holidays.

As you can see, you may have stopped making your own decisions many years earlier because of dominant ex-spouses who effectively made all the choices, whether you approved or not. So, this is also an exciting opportunity to renew yourself.

A good example of this decision making process is the issue of money. In my experience, it is usually one spouse who takes control of the family purse during a marriage and all things *money* go through their decision machine before the allocation of funds is dealt with. On many occasions, their spouse only sees the results of the financial decisions, such as the family home's mortgage balance reducing, a tax bill or credit card debts mounting, rather than any evidence of the thought process at the outset. This is partly because some men believe that money is their domain and not to be interfered with, and partly because some women would prefer that the man deals with the accounting side of family finances. I have certainly witnessed much evidence of this through my work as a financial adviser.

However, after divorce, many people are left with funds from the proceedings and no idea how to use these to their best advantage. As a financial adviser of many years, I have witnessed this situation on frequent occasions in two scenarios, either in the event of divorce or on the death of a spouse, both having their own significant effects on what to do with the household finances.

If you find yourself in this situation, then make sure that you take advice from someone you trust — quickly. Speak to your solicitor or a family member or friend and ask for a recommendation to a financial adviser who is independent. Or you may prefer to use an accountant, depending on your circumstances, to help you manage your money and finances.

A good, well qualified, financial adviser can assess your personal situation, look at your future expectations and your need for income or capital (or in many cases both), and provide some recommendations on where best to spread your money around, usually using the various tax allowances available, to make your money work for you. Any money/advice relationship like this should be based on trust, both now and into the future, so you might want to find out at the outset what the costs are for providing you with this advice for your ongoing security. And most importantly, can you work with this adviser? If the answer is no, then find someone else.

From my own point of view, it is not uncommon for the financial adviser to feel like a surrogate 'spouse' for some clients, undertaking the money role of a previous relationship that has long expired. Their objective is for me to undertake a holistic approach to their finances and I am very proud that I am able to help them accordingly. You will find more information and planning thought on the subject of money in Chapter 7, *Money Matters*.

The past is over

I hope that, for you, the end of the past is a relief. Sure, you have still got some baggage, both physical and psychological, and that will be with you for some time. But the deed of divorce and separation is complete and now the future is all yours. Fantastic! Your very own blank canvas with which to start again. You don't get many opportunities like that. I use the word 'opportunity' correctly, because it is exactly that: your new start and one that, with your blank canvas, you can colour as you like. You might want to refer to your childhood memories to remember how much fun this can be.

The recent past may have some bitterness in it because of the divorce proceedings and I can assure you that as your life moves forward, the memories of these events will subside — sadly, with some of the good memories as well. The legal events of the recent past will need to be overcome before you are able to move forward, but the past should not be entirely forgotten, as you will see in the next chapter.

You know where you have been, where you have come from, what works and does not work for you, which parts have to stay in place — such as staying in work and housing — and what is yours to create. By now, I hope you are also getting an idea of what is going to make you truly comfortable in yourself. If you don't know this, or haven't considered it yet, then start this process now.

Attitude is everything in most things that you do. I was once told that I needed three things in life. They are Attitude, Attitude and Attitude, all of this the 'can do' variety. The language is very 'salesy', but it works. Whilst considering how you want your future to look and exploring the many possibilities, remember that this may be a once in a lifetime opportunity to right some wrongs, and put you back on the track that you may have always wanted to follow. Talk to family and friends about ideas you may have, and start to build your picture.

This opportunity is yours to embrace. You just need to find out what or whom you want to hug!

At the end of each chapter I have left *Your Notes* space for you to think about your personal situation and perhaps scribble down a few thoughts as we progress together through your plan of divorce recovery. This should allow you to consider the points and objectives that matter to you, and how you will begin to structure your plans and approach to your new life.

Your Notes

What opportunities are you looking to fulfil, at the outset of your divorce recovery?

_____

_____

_____

_____

_____

_____

_____

What is the biggest hurdle you face in your recovery?

_____

_____

_____

_____

_____

_____

_____

_____

Nagged, Tagged and Bagged...

Chapter Two

Looking back

The ingredients of you

I hope you are not a person to linger in the past, especially that bit of the past where your divorce lies. However, you are part of the past and it is part of you. The past is a memory, fading and changing over time, with only the highlights glinting in the night sky of your mind. Emotional as these highlights may be, you know how to find these memories: usually when you close your eyes as you drift off to sleep every night.

What we are is merely the sum of the parts that brought us to our current position. Our past is what has shaped us, whether we like it or not. I am not referring to the influence of your ex-spouse or partner, but where you have come from, what you experienced when you grew up, what your parents and school taught you, your education, your ethics or religion, your work, hobbies, your beliefs. These are the ingredients of the rich soup that is you.

Each ingredient is likely to have been provided by an episode in your life that formed a part of you before you moved on to the next phase. Your life is your own evolving story, which grows and grows over time. Like any episode of a television soap opera, with you as the scriptwriter, you can write people in or out, switch locations and move the storyline in whatever direction you want — usually making reference to the action of the previous episodes as you go along.

And like any TV soap, your personally-experienced past, with all its feelings, wonders, lessons, successes and failures, will mould your view on everything that happens to you now and in the future. It is not my intention here to focus particularly on your former relationship, although that may have been a factor while you meandered through memories of this or that decade. What I want to look at are the various life experiences you would have encountered during your journey to the present day.

If you hadn't experienced all those things, good and bad, it is unlikely that you would know what you want going forward. The value of these thoughts will shape your desires as you face your future.

Indeed, some people argue that the reason why websites, such as *Friends Reunited*, are so popular is the desire to retrace one's steps and rekindle relationships from times remembered as being rather better than the present. Many a new (or renewed) relationship has come about from contact with old boyfriends or girlfriends who were also looking back towards lost liaisons. Perhaps that is because of dissatisfaction with their current partners, or because the Internet makes it possible to see through to its proper conclusion a past relationship that may have fizzled out far too early. Such contact can raise the question of whether they took a wrong turn by marrying their present spouse rather than waiting for a *lost beau* to come back into the picture.

In my mind, this brings us back to the reality of life.

Unless you are the lady in the Lear jet at the beginning of the book, life can be a daily grind of paying bills, meeting employers' requirements and other chores. As you cast your mind back, it is easy to remember the highlights that make you smile, while the reality of life's commitments fades into the background. No wonder the grass looks greener than it really was back then.

In fact, life's opportunities are still there for you right now. Turning an opportunity into a reality should be one of your challenges, objectives and wishes. You just have to be careful what you wish for.

In researching this book, I spoke to a few people who declared that they had been 'effectively dead' in their previous marriage, with no life or objective of their own. They had endured many emotions including humiliation, rage, self pity and depression at various times. These were only natural and part of the process for many people in this divorce transition situation. Their lives carried on, although just not in the format that they had hoped for or wanted. The dissolution of their union had in effect been the start of their life, obviously now with much accumulated wisdom, and a chance to develop into the person they finally wanted to be. The delight in their release was tangible, and this new found sense of joy in life will only grow.

If you choose not to believe me, there is a small survey at the end of this chapter that may persuade you otherwise.

Earlier, I talked about a person being no more than the sum of the ingredients that made them. Each person will have different experiences. Next time you start to get involved with someone, ask them what their *ingredients* are and how they made them who they are today. At worst, this should make for an intimate conversation — and remember, you too will have to share *your* story whilst enjoying theirs.

An encounter with me

As we are having some time together in this chapter, I thought I might share some examples of a few of my own *ingredients*, to give you a flavour of who I am and the environments in which I slipped through over various decades. This might jolt a few memories for you, and help shape what you might discover yourself by looking back in order to move forward.

I was born in Oxfordshire. My memory of this is understandably vague for this part of my life because at the age of five the family upsized from its fifties bungalow and moved to Berkshire, and then to Surrey. Personally, a string of houses and wives followed, bringing me up to the present day.

All things new were discovered in Reading in the early seventies and I still have a natural affection for the region and the era. At my young age, the 1970s world was a wonderful place. Our new home was on an early 70's 'Neo-Geo' estate full of tiring psychedelic wallpaper and paint designs. This was the time of Raleigh Chopper bikes, John Travolta in *Grease*, Action Man toys, Space Hoppers, Angel Delight pudding, Green Shield Stamps and always somewhere exciting to explore.

By the 1980s, my family had moved to an older more grandiose house in Surrey and my world slid into the era of big hair, a few O-levels, CSEs (remember them?), Mini Metro cars, microwave ovens, the pop music of George Michael and Wham! and a more affluent world under the auspices of the Thatcher government. Education moved from school to sixth form studying Art and then to work, with adolescent cuddles in the playground evolving to become relationships, whilst watching the film *Mannequin* at the flicks. This was truly a different world to what I had experienced in the mid-seventies in Reading. The grasping of new opportunities, in whatever format and shape they arrived, was my purpose.

By the 1990s, the world had begun to become a smaller and even more exciting place with the advancement of mobile telecommunications. The 'must-have' item was a big black brick called a Cellphone, a 'new' Labour government came into power, and the Internet took off with a bang. I bought my own house with my brother at age twenty one and my parent's home became a weekly Sunday destination to have a 'proper' meal and get some vegetables inside me to stave off any nutritional shortfalls, while my own mortgage costs and take-aways became daily burdens. The perceived benefits and wisdom of the Eighties was being superseded by a decade of Euro Trash and entertainment alternatives such as the animation, *Toy Story*. The age of opportunity was slipping into a world of 'reality', with some hindsight thrown in as an afterthought.

In the next decade, known as the 'noughties', many of us became slaves to mobile telecommunication. Bigger sales targets, mortgage borrowings and marriage followed as we all became victims of a bombardment of information that reached us at any time, day or night, in the office, at home and even on the beach. The world of wizardry came to life with Harry Potter and the horrors of the terror attacks in New York and the second Gulf war set a new context to all our lives.

Personally, there was promotion to chase, company cars, stealth taxes, industry exams and pressure, pressure, pressure. You know the feeling. The reality of life had arrived, bringing with it Laura Ashley wallpaper and discount sofas, with the world of opportunity nothing more than a diminishing memory. Green Shield Stamps were replaced by swipeable Nectar cards, and Space Hoppers by laptop computers. There was one consolation: Nectar cards never give you that vile stamp-glue taste when you lick them to stick in a collection book!

If you don't understand this last joke, enjoy being so young.

Relationships became more serious and committed as they moved to marriages and, in some cases, divorces.

You can see from my notes in this section some of my ingredients and the factors that had a bearing on their involvement that partly creates my receipt.

Life has a habit of taking us all on different journeys, with different people, and each path and environment will create a unique individual, that's what makes us all different. It is important for us all to know what our ingredients are, how we use them and where they came from to help us look to our futures with confidence.

Everywhere you went, and every year that passed by, you met new people and lost contact with others. They drifted in and out of your live, some influencing your future and others dropping away before you really got to know them.

Don't forget people

It is easy to be reminded of people you were with in the past, and often you'll wonder: 'Whatever happened to . . . ?' I am sure you know the feeling. You also know that their loss from your life was nothing personal, just a consequence of life events that may have moved them away, possibly geographically or emotionally. Do you miss them? You may have fond memories of the time and era, but that may be the extent of your thoughts. Time can play tricks with your memory as it fades. This is nothing new and it will continue to happen as long as you live. Even the great friends that you have right now may be consigned to your memory bank in the next decade. This may be a reason why Internet sites, such as Friends Reunited, Facebook and alike have been so popular in being able to retrace contacts with reasonable ease.

Thinking about this a stage further, your contact with those in the past may allow you to take a detached view of where you are now, and how important the people are who make up your current social and work scene now. I hope that there are some that you know who will be there for each remaining decade of your life. There may be others that have already deserted you in the divorce process, and others that you may wish would disappear.

This process will allow you to focus on who is important to you — and, more importantly, to understand why they matter so much. This will also help in creating a strategy for your future with the people you want to be with, learning from what you have experienced in the past. This will shape and mould your views, reactions and actions when looking at the path of your recovery.

An encounter with you

This book is not a one way street; now it's your turn. I have detailed the first exercise for you to consider below when thinking about yourself and the past that shaped you. Tell yourself about you. Where were you born? Where did you move around to? Why there? What did your parents do? Was that good for you? What was school (and university) like for you? Who was your first childhood sweetheart? What happened? Who was your first true love? Why did you/do you work for whoever you work(ed) for? Did you enjoy the 60s/70s/80s/90s? Why? What did you learn?

Exercise

Tell me about you?

How did you locate where you are and why?

What's good for you?

Which decade did you enjoy the most and why?

Extra notes space has been made available at the end of this chapter.

I hope your responses make interesting conversation and a very personal reflection.

Once you have had a good trip through your memories you can start looking forward, possibly in terms of the future decades ahead.

What of the decades that come next? The teens, twenties and thirties? All of them will be different and will change dramatically, as we have already considered in this chapter. Those decades will see significant change from what has gone before. The future should be fascinating and I can't wait to see it.

For memory purposes, you can compartmentalise different experiences and adventures by where they happened. When I do this, I think about the time from the late 1960s to the present day. This allows me to visualise which location I was in, pinpointing the year and the people I would have been with. This can enable more of the memory to come back to me and to remember more of what happened. This is not always the case, but the process can certainly work. Try it for yourself.

Looking back at my own life, some of the moves and changes I made were excellent and I hold much affection for them. Others are darker memories, times I would prefer to forget. However, each event is held in a compartment in my mind, boxed in the past, allowing me to enjoy (or not!) the memory — but then put back in its box while I move on. This leaves me freedom to find new situations, which in turn will be boxed up for the future.

These life phases are parked in my mind for my own understanding, with only the occasional visit for recollection, reminiscence and contemplation. With the benefit of this past wisdom to help guide my future decisions and directions, it's time to move on again with my future.

Memory balance

Sometimes people find that most of the memories they're aware of seem to be negative. Unhappy memories must be balanced by thoughts of the good times, however few these may have been. It does not have to be this way. You still have your future in front of you, and you have some control of how you'll respond to whatever will happen.

Should you find yourself locked in by unhappy memories, then try a balancing exercise. For every poor outcome that you remember, consciously balance it with one good outcome. You may struggle at first, and don't worry if you find it hard at first to find your own balance. However, by pushing yourself through the positive/negative process you will start to balance your memories naturally, simply by *looking* for the good while also noting the negatives.

After a while, I believe you will start to notice your views and highlights taking on a more positive light.

The exercise overleaf may help you with your progression

Exercise

List your main positive memories here

Why are they positive to you?

List your main negative memories here

Why are they negative for you?

Do you remember where you were and who you were with when these memories occurred?

Extra notes space has been made available at the end of this chapter.

I have used the examples of geographical moves and decade time-frames to illustrate how the past can move in phases, but this can be applied to any circumstances. This might be your own or your child's progression through different schools, or through episodes of illness, the situations, influence and possibly problems of those around you, such as relatives, or different jobs and where you commuted to, even where you were with different partners or a past spouse. Remember that human emotions run at their height for issues such as divorce, home moves and employment changes.

Where will this point you?

I hope you enjoyed your personal trip down *memory lane*, lingering to look at the golden fields of happiness and pleasure, made all the more poignant by a fading memory. If you have siblings or friends who were present at a particular point in your past, it is sometimes worth sharing a memory with them to see if their recollection is the same. Their thoughts can be very different and often the sharing can enhance what was already a good memory.

Another way of looking at this is returning to an old holiday haunt that you have not visited for years. The outline and the landscape may well be the same, but the colour, people and atmosphere is likely to have changed out of all recognition, greatly altering your memory perception. Like you, locations alter with time and the landscape that you happily remember strolling around all that time ago may shatter or improve your recollections. It is unlikely that this new situation will inspire you today as it did, if you have fond recollections of it, in the past.

However, returning to our memory balance of positive and negative, many people have bolt-holes around the globe where they disappear to now and then — budget allowing — to be assured of the respite they crave. Marking out some proper 'you' time is always worthwhile. I have one friend who regularly departs to Dubai for warmth and wellbeing. Esther's place is Hong Kong if she ever gets the chance, and this is usually subject to budget constraints. Having been there with her, I can understand the benefits. Others prefer somewhere closer to home and having been *Nagged, Tagged and Bagged*, the finances may dictate this. This will always be a deeply personal choice.

In the exercises above we have looked at what ingredients, positive and negative, have made you who you are today, and may provide some guide as to the way you will be in the future.

In thinking about the points raised in this chapter, have you decided what your ingredients, both positive and negative, are with the memory jogging of people, places and experiences that have created the personality that is now you? Have you decided what's involved in you? Possibly, more importantly, do you know your recipe, how you are put together? What's the main flavour of you? The list of possibilities is endless, with examples such as strong, educated, robust, calm, lovable, warm, charming or shy. We are all a mix of various traits and styles and these are created from your experiences.

List your thoughts in the next exercise.

Exercise

List your main ingredients, styles and traits here

_____

_____

_____

How did your experiences create the ingredients of you?

_____

_____

_____

_____

Which is your best ingredient and your least used?

_____

_____

_____

_____

Which would you like to develop more?

_____

_____

_____

Extra notes space has been made available at the end of this chapter.

I hope these helped you think more about you and with your *ingredients* in place, you should start to have a flavour of what you want the future to hold for you. If you are still unsure of what made you who you are, then have another look at the text and exercises above. These will obviously be thoughts and ideas from your past and this does not mean that you are going to head straight back to square one and repeat what has gone before. On the contrary, it gives you the advantage of knowing where you came from, what worked for you, what is best for you and where you are most comfortable. This may allow you to miss out unprofitable repetitions this time around. Also, the past should give you confidence for the future. This does not mean that you will find guaranteed happiness and peace in the future — but you are more likely to be facing the right direction to find something closer to what you had anticipated.

I hope that the reflection on your past inspires you for your future. If you are sharing your thoughts of the past with someone else, do listen carefully to their responses to what you are saying. Also, many of the wisest comments also come from within yourself; you just have to listen.

Two questions

Having sewn my thoughts and views of past and present into the fabric of this text, I thought a bit of private research might be in order, to give you the context for my reminiscences and anecdotes.

I had spoken and communicated to a few friends and contacts who had been through the divorce process and come out on the other side, still breathing and with a shirt (or blouse) on their backs. People do survive and thrive after divorce. It's not a myth, as you will soon see.

To keep things simple, I asked each of them the same two questions. The individuals that I asked were aware that I was writing this book and understood my objectives, although I did not offer them any other guidance than the questions to obtain their individual feelings. I have maintained anonymity to protect their identities — however, I would like to take this opportunity to thank them for sharing their innermost thoughts.

My questions were as follows:

- Thinking about your divorce, what was the one thing that really surprised you in the process?

- If there was one main benefit of the outcome of your divorce, what would it be?

You may have guessed that I was expecting one negative response and one positive response (in that order) from each question. How wrong I was.

Before going further, you might like to ask yourself the same questions, to see what responses you would give before reading the answers I received. Try it, it won't take long.

The exercise overleaf may help you with your progression

Exercise

What was the one thing that really surprised you in your divorce process?

_____

_____

_____

What was your one main benefit of your divorce?

_____

_____

_____

Extra notes space has been made available at the end of this chapter.

Returning to my questions, I received the following replies:

Thinking about your divorce, what was the one thing that really surprised you in the process?

The answers received were as follows:

'The steep learning curve (for the proceedings) was amazing . . . I didn't expect it to take so long.'

'Finding out that the problem in the marriage was me, not them.'

'It was almost as though I was mourning the death of a loved one. So much so, I felt sick every morning I woke up. This continued for at least six months after my divorce. I wanted this divorce, had dreamt of my 'freedom' *for years. This was not what I was supposed to feel . . . no one ever warned me of this! Oh my God . . . had I made a mistake?'*

'I didn't expect the revenge and nastiness from the other side. That was a big surprise.'

'I felt that my marriage had stolen my real identity. The struggle to regain my maiden name and to update my banking facilities, etc, was a nightmare. Men know nothing of this!'

'The biggest surprise, after the initial shock and emotional turmoil [of making the decision to divorce], was I was surprised how simple and amicable the whole process has been, even with significant financial assets and children involved. I put this down to the two individuals involved, rather than the divorce process itself.'

'How easy the divorce process was!'

You can tell that the individual circumstances of each divorce process and its smooth or troubled passage created a very different outcome, which influenced the point at which the individual's personal recovery started. It is interesting to also see the style of the various quotes. I would suggest that you should take this into account when planning your way forward. Some people may find the point of their start to recover easier than others.

Turning to the second question below, the responses were equally varied:

If there was one main benefit of the outcome of your divorce, what would it be?

The answers received were as follows:

'I found out who I was and was able to breathe again.'

'There was a sense of relief that it was over. The surprise was that this was almost instant.'

'The divorce allowed me to step back and evaluate what was important to me, to understand what I wanted to achieve in life and what I wanted to spend my time doing.'

'The recovery of my self-esteem and confidence and without sounding like a therapist . . . I found me again . . . exactly what I had hoped and dreamed of for so long. Was it a mistake? Certainly not!'

'The divorce has bought me a lot closer to my children and we now spend more quality time together.'

'I learned what mattered in terms of possessions. Like others coming to maturity, I thought a lot of life was about getting the house, the car, the nice kitchen equipment and even the right wedding presents. When we split everything in two, and I lost things that I felt were mine and that mattered to me, merely to stop another argument, I started to feel liberated. I rarely stress about possessions any more; I focus much more on people. And I don't look backwards, only forwards. If my house burned down tomorrow, with everything I own in it, I wouldn't care.'

'In this way, it has been a gift of clarity and I am surprisingly grateful for that.'

'The divorce has made me more selective about my relationships, whereas before I was rarely single for more than a couple of weeks.'

'I really enjoy making my own choices now.'

'I got to keep the house!' (You can probably guess that this was a male response.)

Without exception, all the responses were thought-provoking, powerful, and were clearly personal to each respondent. I hope they compare with your thoughts. What was also noticeable was that what once had clearly been a very trying and difficult situation and subject, was now water under the bridge; chatting about its effects had become discussing nothing more than a period in life and now a memory.

This was one of the most enjoyable parts of constructing this book. You can tell from the level of the responses that this was not extensive research, but it does give a flavour of other people's honest views on where they started their journey — and, in hindsight, what the benefit of that divorce recovery has been.

It is interesting that none of the respondents thought that there was no benefit at all from their own recovery. Quite the contrary. Asking them to tell me the 'one' main benefit was unsuccessful most of the time, and that has to be a good sign. For some, the list of benefits and opportunities was endless. Thank you again to these people for their input, which has added great value and perspective.

As you can see, some people just need to find themselves. And they did so, very quickly after the separation.

Washing off the past

The past is over now, and only the future is available to you and me. However, the ability to reflect on the past to summarise its lessons, and to draw a line under them, allows us each to move forward with greater confidence and self esteem.

Finding yourself, after the mayhem that has gone before, can happen very quickly for some. Others will take longer. As mentioned in the introduction, finding yourself is a '*Life Junction*'. You know *where* you are, you know where you have *been* and now you just need to decide where you want to *go*. The crossroads before you will beckon you left, right or dead-ahead. As the responses above show, many of the people I spoke to stepped outside their comfort zone to go forward — not necessarily from choice. Whichever direction they headed in, and remember it was their own decision, none of them was disappointed.

If you are at this *Life Junction*, go with confidence. Yes, it may look scary. Life and Sat Navs have already taught you that a wrong turn is possible. But this experience will only teach you which the right way is.

Your Notes

List your key experiences, people, places and learning points from the past.

Which are your best ingredients and which are the ones you would like to improve?

Chapter Three

Signposts

There is no magic wand you can wave to speed up divorce recovery.

Some people are lucky and land on their feet every time. My wife, Esther, is one of these people. Her mother suggests that Esther has nine lives, and it doesn't matter where you drop her from, she will always make the best of it. Have you ever noticed how this appears to happen to certain 'lucky' types? Annoying as this may be, you can engineer your own luck. You just need to know how.

A tight-fisted customer once said to his newsagent: 'If only I could win the Lottery.'

The newsagent's reply was 'Improve your chances, buy a ticket!'

As the lottery's strap line suggests, *you've got to be in it to win it* — and this is true of everything you want to achieve in life. If you want to find love, you need to start socialising and dating. If you want to move up the employment ladder you need to network with your colleagues or take an exam or two. If you want good health you may need to eat sensibly and exercise more.

Again, no magic wand here, just energy focused on what you want to achieve. This is exactly what those 'lucky' people do: they think ahead and are prepared.

How prepared do you need to be? Where does this planning start and stop?

Future mapping

Many people, when first released from a marriage, live a hand-to-mouth, almost feral, existence while they get used to their new circumstances. At this stage, many people do not want to plan — either because they are not in a hurry, or because they are still recovering from the divorce they have just been through. Sometimes it is simply that they can't be bothered, which after all they have been through, is a fair response. After all, they'd had everything mapped out before their marriage breakdown and a fat lot of good that did them.

However, it is worth bracing yourself to start planning ahead. I'm sure you have some ideas as to what's going to happen in the next few months and where you're going to be. The mortgage or tenancy agreement may dictate the location, or the confines of your work role may also influence where you live and your view of what is an acceptable time commute each day, if that is what you have to do.

In this chapter, I want to talk about the longer term, say the next five, ten, fifteen years, even into and past retirement. Remember some of the dreams you used to have? Although a divorce has got in the way of these aspirations, possibly emotionally as well as financially, it is possible to rebuild a vision — *your* vision, to be precise — of how it is going to look for you in the future.

One easy way of achieving this is by signposting your path forward.

Emotional signposts

Signposts usually tell you where you are going, but they aren't always easy to read or recognise. These signposts can be in varying formats. One might be a signpost in time, such that when you reach it you will want something particular to happen. Or you might have emotional signposts, which signal where you are in your recovery programme.

During the emotional recovery stage, you may go through a kaleidoscope of emotions. With your world apparently in freefall, you may feel *obsession*, *depression* and *anxiety* about why the previous relationship failed. This in turn may cause you some *guilt* as you reflect on the past. Guilt can then lead to *regret*. You know that the old relationship is over and trying to apologise may not be appropriate after all that has happened; it may be best to leave the past in the past. The benefit of this hindsight is that you have the chance to learn the lessons that any mistakes can teach you, if indeed, they were mistakes.

Another commonly-experienced emotion is *anger*. This needs to be handled with care and controlled if necessary. You may feel anger at your ex-spouse or partner, or anger at your new and possibly unwanted situation. You may be at a point of loneliness and even bitterness. Trying to even the score is not going to work and the energy you will waste dwelling on this point should instead be channelled into your positive future. Being polite with your ex-spouse for child contact purposes will be more supportive to your children, both now and in their future development, and this will help both you and them in return. You don't want them to become bargaining chips in a battle between parents.

Remember that in your married life together, there were good *and* bad times with your ex-spouse. These phases will naturally occur again in your separated lives. Make sure you build some understanding of this into your outlook.

It is also important to remember that you are not alone in your new, possibly single, circumstances. Getting to meet and enjoy new people is only a matter of making the effort to go and find them.

Going through these emotions may lead to *frustration*. Frustration in itself can be wasted energy. It tempts you to dwell on the past, when you want to concentrate on your path to freedom from the old you. You will need focus, desire and determination to ensure that the positives — and there are positives — come out of all those feelings.

Time signposts

Time signposts might be an easy and more tangible way of following your process of divorce recovery. You can map and mark on a calendar where you want to be and when you want to have achieved your objectives. If you need to, buy or even make a calendar with dates going forward for a few years. Then you can plot important landmarks on the calendar and visualise where you want to be at those points in time. You may think this is just dreaming. Ask yourself this: if you can't have dreams and aspirations, what can you have? Both hope and desire *start* with dreams. You would not be able to fly in a plane today if the Wright Brothers had not had dreams of putting people into the sky. The telephone call you made last was only possible because of the dreams, inovations and inspiration of Alexander Graham Bell.

I always think it's worth thinking about a big event in the future and asking where you want to be when that event happens. This could be anything from the Olympics in 2020 to that big birthday, say in 2025, or a growing child's 'gap year' before going to university, as examples. You can almost use these dates as a target of where you want to be in your development, such as re-marriage with a new family, or relocated, possibly in a new job, or even just content as a single individual.

You can use this process for any personal target, from reaching a target weight after a diet, passing a test, doing a bungee jump — you name it. Your targets will be personal to you and your circumstances. Think about an event that you are likely to attend in the future, your child's graduation ceremony, or that 40th/50th/60th birthday. When you are sitting at the celebration, enjoying the moment, you will have wanted to . . . only you can fill in the gap.

You will then need to work backwards from what you have marked in the future, to ensure that you put in place the relevant stepping stones now to reach your targets.

As I often say, we are all individuals running individual lives with individual desires. Therefore each target will be personal to *you*. And if you don't hit them, it should be appropriate to ask why not? Has your desire to reach your target, and possibly inner peace, subsided? If it has, you could argue that you only have yourself to blame. Some people find that their initial targets do change over time. This can happen with the introduction of new people in their lives, who open up new and unexpected opportunities beyond their wildest dreams.

There are many names for this process. You could call it 'future mapping', or 'your lifeline' or anything you like.

However, before you can look to the future, you must be able to know who you are now and what you have to offer to achieve your goals.

Who are you?

Who are you? It might seem an odd question, but ask yourself anyway. I hope you like your answer, because you need to know this.

Take a moment to think about this question and the honest truth of the answers. At this point, you might want to use the exercise or notes section at the end of this chapter to list your all of your virtues and one or two of your shortcomings, which, as we are all only human, all have.

In your outlook, is your glass half full or half empty?

In your needs, are you demanding or easy going?

In your virtues, are you kind and outgoing, feisty and gregarious or, alternatively, insular and difficult to connect with?

These are only examples and there are no right or wrong answers. In thinking about this you will understand that this list could be endless. However, if you don't know the real you, it is unlikely anyone else is going to be able to find out about the real you.

If you were able to come up with a realistic answer, how did you reach your conclusion? Are you happy and comfortable within yourself with the answer you have given? Now that your circumstances have changed, hopefully for the better, and usually with more personal freedom, does the answer match your expectations for the future? Use the exercise below to help with your thoughts.

Exercise

Tell me about your virtues and outlook?

Tell me about your shortcomings and development points?

How did you come to your answers?

Do your answers match your expectations for your future?

Extra notes space has been made available at the end of this chapter.

As we grow older we should grow wiser. It's important to understand how you are going to evolve and grow further in your new and hopefully improved future. I realise that _new and improved_ sounds like a detergent advert, but hopefully after the 'spin cycle' of divorce emotions that you have just been through, you will come out of the whole experience looking, feeling and thinking better.

What did you learn from the divorce proceedings? It can be difficult to walk away from them without thinking you must be a modern day devil, considering all the marital crimes you've supposedly committed. The reality is that this is just the divorce _process_; you need to remember your virtues too.

Most people do not have to look far to know what makes a person interesting, attractive, witty and generally great to have around. If you start to struggle with your self esteem — and it would be understandable, after having the spotlight of negative appraisal shining on you — then talk to your best friend or a close relative about every aspect of you, and believe what they tell you. No fibbing now!

Clearly there will be some honesty in this conversation. It needs to cover what's great, what works for you, and also those areas you might want to consider avoiding. (For example, I can be quite strong willed and this can appear opinionated.)

Once you know your successes, virtues and areas to avoid, you can start to look forward to how you are going to use these things to your advantage. This will lead you to being more complete and fulfilled in yourself.

Finding peace

It is my firm belief that, if you plan for the future using whatever assets you have, great or small, you will find peace. The only question is: what would *peace* look like to you?

This might be with a partner or a new spouse. Or it might be simply contentment on your own. Being on your own does not mean being lonely; it could mean a large social network and enjoying a variety of activities and encounters, without the burden of another party as a partner.

The exercise overleaf may help you with your progression

Exercise

Tell me what peace looks like to you?

Why is this your answer?

Extra notes space has been made available at the end of this chapter.

Some people use social media networks, such as Bebo, Myspace and Twitter to keep in contact with friends and also to locate and contact old acquaintances that may have fallen by the wayside over the years. There are those who suggest that these contact sites have actually been the cause of marriage breakdowns, and many people see them as a threat because of this.

Starting new relationships

First of all, let's not forget that being single can be great fun and if that suits you then go with it.

If it does not suit you, then you need to know you are unlikely to get it right first time when you start dating again. It's like being back in the playground and playing 'kiss chase'. Once you have got your 'kiss', or whatever it is you were hoping to get in adult terms, you may decide that what you were chasing after was not what you wanted.

Don't forget to take into account that it may have been years, if not decades, since you went out on a date and the world has moved on since the social etiquette that you learned all those years ago. There is more on the subject of etiquette later in the book.

The good news is that, once you play the dating game for a little while, you start to home in on what you are really looking for. At this stage, progress might be a matter of better timing, or identifying the right person, or finding peace in yourself to have the confidence to start again; only you will know what the key factors are. However, it is easy to become dejected if you have a few false starts, so you need to remind yourself that these are only natural.

Relationships are like learning to ride a bicycle: you never forget once you have learned, but that does not mean you can't fall off a few times. And the faster you go, the more painful it is when you have an accident.

Esther looks at it another way. She says: *'you have to kiss many frogs to find a Prince . . . and watch out for the toads!'*

She also suggests that old habits die hard. If you were highly irritated by your old partner leaving the toilet seat up or squeezing the toothpaste tube in the middle or slurping their coffee, then the reality is that if any new partner starts doing the same things the outcome for you may be exactly the same. It might be a good test of your new partner to tell them that it really annoys you; if they simply ignore the point, they might unconsciously be sending you a negative message. Observe carefully!

These examples might seem like petty grievances, but little things like these can grow into bigger problems when they're added together. Make sure you take this into account if you are looking for a suitable future partner. These standards will guide you in identifying whether someone else can maintain the standards, either high or low, that you expect in a relationship.

Let's move on to the bigger and more important questions. Assuming you have started to see new people, do you know what you are looking for?

Would you say that the people you have dated or socialised with are exact opposites of your past partner or spouse? Is an almost allergic reaction pointing you in the opposite direction to where you have been before? You need to understand what you *did* enjoy about a previous relationship as well as what made you leave or made it break down in the end. You may just be investigating your options and being open-minded to the possibilities, which is great, but do make sure you know which way you are heading and that you are comfortable with this direction.

Again, if we return to the quote on the back cover of this book in which Henry Ford suggests that mistakes are a good thing because they allow you to start again, remember, you may not get it right first time. If you are too specific at the outset about what you want in a future partner, to make sure you don't get it wrong again, this might mean a few things. Firstly, there may be a good reason why your spouse left you, or you left them. Secondly, you need to take a step back and lighten up a bit, in order to be ready to explore your new horizons.

You can be sure that your ex-spouse will be going through the same process, and he or she may fall at the first few hurdles, too.

Internet dating

As I tap away on my computer, using the Internet to verify facts, you can tell that I am no technophobe, whatever Esther might tell you to the contrary. Like many people, when I first went dating, the Internet was in its infancy; therefore, using it as a tool to find love and companionship is an alien concept. However, the world keeps changing and social networking sites have for many people become the norm of social interaction. So, is this the death of personal interaction? Of course not. I believe it is an addition to our networking opportunities, rather than a replacement.

You may be aware of various sites offering different introduction services, opportunities, prices and processes. If you are going to use these facilities, first of all make a few comparisons before you commit. You need to make sure that the service you are buying suits your needs and your budget. If you get it wrong, you could find yourself looking for a loving relationship on a private escort site!

To expand this further, there are now many Internet dating websites that allow you to compare and contrast your compatibility with other individuals, meet online, communicate and, if appropriate, finally meet up. The meeting allows you to verify your understanding of the other person, so you can either continue getting to know them or politely say goodbye and move on. I have heard of many successful unions and marriages using this method, and it has become an everyday part of the process in ever increasing numbers, rather than an oddity. I am reminded of the saying: *'you get what you pay for'*, and you may want to consider this with any website offer you are going to use.

Some people are broadminded in their requirements in a partner, open to many opportunities and adventures to find out or remind themselves of what they do and don't like. This is fine. Others are highly specific, even detailing the minimum academic qualifications that they require even to entertain a suitor. We are all different.

Whether or not you approve of these websites (and remember that they are usually money-making profit centres), they will make you think about what you have got to offer and what you are looking for. The more specific you are – the less likely you are to be disappointed. However, as the saying goes *'be careful what you wish for because you might just get it!'* Sometimes that's not such a good thing.

Security

In the main, dating websites provide good opportunities to get out and meet like-minded people. Many people meet their new spouse this way. However, as with any blind date, always keep your personal security in mind and make sure someone else knows who you are meeting and where. This might make you feel like a child again, telling Mum or Dad which party you are going to (although you don't go armed with a cheap bottle of cider this time), but it's a sensible precaution all the same.

As an additional precaution, make sure that where you first meet is a public, neutral venue. You may want to plan so that this first meeting is not on your doorstep, so that if things don't work out you are unlikely to bump into that person again.

Finally, for my 'concerned parent' section of this book, if you are hoping to have sexual intercourse on the first date, make sure you take a condom with you. I'll explain further in the chapter entitled *Health and Wellbeing*. You will know that sexually transmitted diseases (STDs) are not age limited.

Friendly intrusions

For those who love and care about you, the intrigue of a new *special person* in your life will be hard to hide. They will want to know everything about them before they meet, and then repeat the interrogation once they do meet. They may have been the conduits that first allowed you to meet, without knowing much about their involvement.

You might want to consider taking your time before introducing him or her to friends and family, to make sure of this new growing love or companionship before anyone else gets the chance to intrude; this is especially true for any children you have. It is reasonably easy for anyone to turn on the charm for the first few meetings, only for you to find out later that they are a complete nightmare. You would not want to put your children through the stress of meeting a string of potential suitors until you were satisfied in your own mind that the relationship was going somewhere; it would be unfair to everyone involved otherwise.

Friends may put you under some pressure to meet up or go out on a date together — and this might be a good move, phased over a period. It is certainly a good way of getting another opinion if you want one, especially if you hope to be firm friends later.

This situation will of course be true for you, too, when *you* are ready to meet *your* new partner's friends and family. If they have children then you need to understand that you are possibly taking on more than one person; this may also be the case with your own family.

Your friends are doomed

Just when you thought that the divorce had cost you enough friends, as those not so close to you scattered, falling in love again may have the same effect.

You might think that this is just my own experience and it won't happen to you. However, a study published in autumn 2010 by Oxford University Researchers suggests that falling in love comes at the cost of losing two close friends. Robin Dunbar, Professor of Evolutionary Anthropology at Oxford suggests that, having studied 540 participants over 18 years old, that a new relationship leads to a smaller support network, usually losing one family member and one friend when a new lover appears on the scene, stating: *'The intimacy of a relationship — your emotional engagement with it — correlates very tightly with the frequency of your interactions with those individuals.'*

As noted in the last chapter, the *'What ever happened to ....?'* question starts to ring true and makes you realise that those around you now, those close friends, may not be around in the future simply because you find new love.

So, if some of your friends seem to take a backward step when a new love arrives on the scene, it is nothing personal, just a natural progression.

Take your time, and I hope that any new partner will want to take their time as well, in introducing each other around to friends and family. You don't want your children saying: *'Is this our new mummy/daddy?'* every time you are seen with someone new.

Success is around the corner

It does not take a genius to work out that planning ahead, mapping where you want to be and meeting potential new partners is going to result in some mistakes along the way. Getting it wrong is, in a way, part of the excitement of the process. Please don't beat yourself up if a flourishing relationship unexpectedly collapses, with the intoxication of love being washed away in a phone call or over a quick coffee.

You may well fail to hit an emotional target that you have set yourself. All aspects of life are like that. If this happens then learn from the experience, what went right and what went wrong. Add this data to your armoury of emotional wisdom and move on. Dwelling on your mistakes will only slow your progress; it's more productive to remember the good times you had, instead.

Eventually, you will get it right. Success is likely to be just around the corner for you — it's just that you might have to turn a few corners first until you come to the right point and position.

Your Notes

Consider your future plans, objectives and timings for your aspirations in the future here:

How will you recognise the 'Signposts' and 'Life Junctions' that will guide you?

How will you recognise your success?

Nagged, Tagged and Bagged...

Chapter Four

Stress

You are free from the shackles of the last relationship and your time is now your own. It's true that you may have less money than you started with, and that the only benefactors of the whole divorce process seem to be the solicitors (and barristers, if you had to go that far). But all the same, you are out the other end of the tunnel with, hopefully, more wisdom. A new start beckons.

Running through the checklist of what you need, you will probably have a roof over your head — although it may not be the roof you had hoped for. You have some money in your bank account and a bit of cash in your wallet or purse. You have your health, a yearning to start your life again and to go out and explore.

Although it may not be obvious in the frantic rush to sort your life out, the most important of these items to your future is, in fact, your health. Without it, any dreams and expectations that you have to move forward may be scuppered.

Living in the shadows

After all the issues of the divorce are over, you may just want to lie low for a while to catch your breath and have some quality time all to yourself. I think this is very worthwhile, even if it puts you out of circulation from your friends and relatives for a while. You are not being anti-social, just biding your time until you are ready to re-launch yourself. It's up to you how and when this is achieved.

This may also be partly the result of having low self esteem, a reaction to the failure of a relationship and concerns about the views of others after the divorce is completed. This is an understandable and natural reaction — however, make sure you don't let it swamp you. Excessive self pity is going to get you nowhere.

Lying low can be worthwhile, but some people leave it so long that they lose the knack for getting back into circulation.

Some friends will try to coax you out of your shell. To some extent this is admirable.

You need to understand that you are living in the shadow of your former self; and that person, the former you, is now long gone. We are beginning to establish what the *new* you looks like.

Personally, I remember lying low for a while because of the constraints of my budget, which can be a major factor for many. What with train fares, rent payments, food costs, along with other commitments, that budget was finely balanced; if I could squeeze out a bottle of

'Vino' from the local corner store at the end of the week, I considered myself lucky. However, on a positive note, this new found austerity allowed me to re-focus on what was important to me.

As I will say again later in this book, money can be recovered, but time can't. So, if you find yourself having to curtail your social life due to your budget, think of this as a temporary suspension of frivolity rather than assuming that 'this is what it's going to look like for the rest of my life'. You are *not* doomed. It's just part of the process and once the dust has settled further, you will be able to move forward again.

I do have to add one word of caution to the notes above, and this is not to leave your re-launch too long.

As a discipline, you might want to plan to go out at least once a week — or if you're naturally less sociable, once a month — to make sure you remember that there is a life out there, and that it's just waiting for you to grab it.

Let's face it: the divorce that you have just been through may have been the most stressful thing that you have ever endured. The ever-present fallout from the divorce (a house move, a job change, a renegotiation of your finances) will have also taken their toll on your wellbeing. This combination of factors has been studied, and stress from 'life events' are known to be contributing factors to illness.

Your overall health and wellbeing are vital to your development and plans. Therefore, do not underestimate the effects of what you have been through.

Stress testing

The psychology of stress and its effects on health is a significant subject and one that has been studied and documented. A good example of this subject is a US study called *the Holmes & Rahe Stress Scale* (which for the academics among you is also known as the *Social Readjustment Rating Scale*, or SRRS), which lists no fewer than 43 stressful life events that can contribute to illness, on a relative scale.

In their study of over 5,000 people in 1967, *Holmes & Rahe* concluded that for adults, the top three ranked life events were:

- Death of a spouse

- Divorce

- Marital separation

For adults, each life event was given a stress score and these various events, with a diverse range of situations, such as Christmas, pregnancy and retirement, can be combined to give an individual an overall score.

Adding your own personal life events together creates an overall score, and the higher the score on the scale, the higher the health risk. Using the scale provided, if you score over 300 points then you are 'at risk of illness'. A score below 150 would suggest that you have only a slight risk of illness.

Using the scale provided by the study, it is suggested that if you get divorced, take on a new larger mortgage to re-home yourself, possibly change your living conditions because of your reduced financial state, and then have a few problems at work, you could see your combined score exceeding 150, which, according to the study, would mean you facing an increased risk of illness.

'Illness' can come in many forms, from headaches to weight loss or gain, from losing the ability to organise yourself to skin complaints or even a heart attack. The list is endless and can be potentially life threatening. In your programme of development, make sure you look out for yourself and your circumstance to check for physical and significant emotional changes that may occur.

Some of those forty three life events are more unavoidable than others, mainly because Christmas comes around every single year. Others can be moderated or understood in advance, to ensure their effects are kept as much as possible under control.

As interesting as it is that these situations have been plotted against a scale to demonstrate the potential for illness, it doesn't cover the day-to-day anguish that people going through this change may feel. Again, this needs to be understood at the outset.

As you will be only too aware, when you are going through a divorce, change is coming and it has your name on it. But many people, including myself, would argue that change brings opportunity; and opportunity can create the ability for you to build a new model for your life. I hope that you are attracted to the 'new you'.

If you could change everything, would you? What would you change? Your job, home, location, religion, clothes, social circle, hobbies, car, or just *everything*?

Some people do just that, wiping the slate clean to start again. There is nothing wrong with this if that's what works for them. If you were going to make sweeping changes, in which order would you change them? What would be your top priority and your lowest priority? Try listing out your planned changes below or at the notes section at the end of this chapter. You will have to be honest with yourself as many people are creatures of habit, even if these habits are bad and this may confuse what your real desires are for the future.

Exercise

Tell me about your planned changes?

_____

_____

_____

How would you prioritise these?

_____

_____

_____

Why is your top priority the one you have given?

_____

_____

_____

Extra notes space has been made available at the end of this chapter.

Recovering individuals often change many things, almost as a reaction to their old life, a statement to confirm that they can live again. *Good for them* is my reaction.

Think about the day you'll have tomorrow. What does it contain, other than the stress of paying the rent, maintenance or your next mortgage repayment, meeting your sales target or project deadline, making sure that you reach work on time or the children are at school with the right kit for games lessons or getting that delivery made? It's all pressure!

When did you first realise that you were under pressure? Ten years ago, fifteen or even longer?

Sadly, pressure is a modern phenomenon that is continually tightening its grip on society, in all walks of life. You need to accept this as you plan ahead.

Studies and statistics

The journal, *Stress*, in the summer of 2010, published research by Chicago University into single people and couples and their respective stress situations. The study found that people who were together as a couple produced fewer stress related hormones than those who were single. Marriage *'has a dampening effect on Cortisol (a steroid hormone) responses to psychological stress,'* suggests Professor Dario Maestripieri in his analysis.

He continues by suggesting that single and unpaired individuals are more responsive to psychological stress than married individuals, and that this is consistent with growing evidence from other research that marriage and social support can be a *buffer* against stress. The Chicago University study takes further the outcomes of other studies that have found that married couples live longer and have less heart disease and other health issues.

As a possible alternative confirmation of these study findings, The Office of National Statistics for England and Wales found that single mothers and widowed men suffer the worst health, with the greatest level of both chronic and acute conditions. Wives with children are the healthiest. Single men between the ages of 30 and 59 are two and a half times more likely to die than their married counterparts.

You may be thinking that you did not need a study from a university in America or the UK statisticians to tell you it's more stressful to be on your own. I would have to agree with you. From a personal point of view, it is great to have someone to bounce ideas off or to chat through consequences — but not at any cost, as you too have found.

The studies available suggest that our personal chemistry responds less well to being single. Whilst you are thinking about this, you may want to tink about others close to you.

Stress can be experienced by children as well.

Stress in young people

Don't you think that your children and teenagers are likely to suffer stress in the process of divorce and afterwards? The reason for introducing the subject of children and stress at this stage is that the study by Holmes & Rahre, noted under the sub heading *Stress Testing*, also looks at the stress points for non-adults.

The stress scale was modified and applied to young people. Featuring various 'life events' applicable for young people, the scale includes unwed pregnancy and acquiring a visible deformity. With this new scale, one of the highest scorers on this scale is *the divorce of parents* along with *the marital separation of parents*. The charity RELATE confirms that studies show that parents who share the care of the children from the marriage are able to help children to cope better with the strains of the division (source: *www.relate.org.uk*).

The care and maintenance of children is a specialist subject. If you have any doubts about the wellbeing of your own children, seek professional advice as soon as possible to ensure that you are looking after their physical as well as their mental health. You may want to speak to your doctor or to RELATE, for example. There are other organisations that can help children directly, such as Childline, which is designed for children up to the age of eighteen.

Bear in mind that children will have more than enough stress of their own to deal with as they move through puberty, adolescence, education and into the work environment. Their years of youth should not be cluttered with separated parents sniping at each other at every opportunity. If you are still in contact with your children — and sadly, many separated parents are not — make sure you do all you can to keep your relationship with your ex-spouse on a mature and adult basis to give the children of the marriage some peace. More on this subject later.

The same scale for the potential of stress causing illness applies to this modified study for young people as it does for the standard adult study. Again, using the scale, over

300 points places the non-adult 'at risk of illness'. The difference I have noted in this new scale is that the 'life events' seem to be more immediate, such as a parent starting work or a brother or sister leaving home. To an adult, this may seem like a natural and obvious life progression, but to a youngster it can be an addition to a stress level that may already be high because of the events of a separation and divorce.

For this modified scale, the categories suggested are a real eye-opener about how stress in the young can accumulate so quickly. Think about this carefully with your own children and take prompt action if appropriate.

Make sure that you monitor the health situations of you and your loved ones regularly, to ensure that you can all maintain the course of your aspirations.

Thinking ahead

Change can bring great opportunity, but this may come hand in hand with some stress. If you have children and are thinking of changing significant parts of your life after a divorce, then do take into account the stress that the effects of your decisions will have on the children and young people of the household.

You and your loved ones health is an important subject and I have looked at health and wellbeing in greater depth in the next chapter. The thoughts and comments in the next chapter may help you with some aspects of stress.

Your Notes

Identify what is causing you concern and stress at the moment.

List your ways of helping and overcoming any stress you feel.

Nagged, Tagged and Bagged...

Chapter Five

Health and wellbeing

We talked about *lucky people* earlier, and noted how they always seem to land on their feet. When it comes to health, you will also meet the same 'lucky' types that can eat for England and never put any weight on, or who smokes like a chimney and still beat you round a squash court between cigarettes. This is annoying at the best of times, especially if you are naturally at the other end of the health and wellbeing scale.

Again, you will know your sort: the mere thought of a slimline cracker makes you put on a pound in weight and break into a sweat putting on your gym shorts, let alone play a game of tiddlywinks. I tend to fall into this latter category, as you may have gathered, and it is only a question of *how much* weight I put on, rather than *whether* I put it on.

During my recovery from divorce, this fact focused my mind on being fit enough to survive the process and, more importantly, to have the energy to prosper afterwards. Good health is essential to your re-development.

Health and nutrition

Good health will not be found at the bottom of a wine or beer glass, although it may have had a soothing effect whilst reading all those solicitors' letters during the course of your matrimonial proceedings. Neither will consuming takeaways every night, either because you can't be bothered, or possibly because you don't know how to cook — but mainly because there is only you and 'it's a real fag cooking every night'.

Being on first name terms with the local curry house is nothing to be proud of, however tasty it seems.

Right from the start of your new single life, you need to be able to cater for yourself and your family. Giving yourself a balanced and healthy diet will help your body stay trim and your wallet stay plump from the savings you make. Start with a trip to the supermarket to stock up your fridge or freezer compartment. If you are single and struggling to find the time to cook, then make a meal for two; once the surplus half has completely cooled, cover it and put it in the fridge for reheating the next day. Make sure you follow all the relevant health guidelines so that your reheated culinary masterpiece doesn't make you ill.

Try swapping a takeaway for a meal suggestion from a cookbook once in a while. It's about the same cost and you never know, you might find out that you enjoy cooking!

First impressions

Wellbeing also affects your personal appearance.

It's tempting to get lazy about this in the recovery stage, especially if you kept your looks to a high standard before the separation. There is little pleasure to be had in looking scruffy, which may be a reflection of how you are feeling inside, and it will be noticed by old and new acquaintances alike. Your appearance may be seen as embodying your own general wellbeing. I don't mean the odd 'wardrobe crisis' you may suffer before going to some social event, but how you tend to look every day and the attention you pay yourself.

For example, a man might not bother to shave or iron his shirt properly. A person could put on a few extra pounds in weight and not mind too much about it. During the stress of the divorce process, you may have suffered some weight loss, when the only thing you ate at certain meal times was the unpalatable contents of a solicitor's letter. Recovering some of that weight may make you feel better and, if you lost a lot of weight, look better. But keep it under control and take medical advice if it's going too far.

I understand that just a regular good night's rest might be just the tonic to help, although this may be easier said than done at the outset. They don't call it *beauty sleep* for nothing!

Other examples might be not polishing your shoes as often, or not having your hair cut or coloured regularly. Whatever the presentation issue is, make sure that you maintain your personal grooming standards. However, if your personal standards were naturally low, you might want to review them, taking into account your clothes and personal hygiene. In writing these comments, I feel like a parent setting rules for a child — however, these standards do apply to your situation and you should be aware of what is acceptable to the real you, and what isn't.

Regular exercise

Pushing a trolley around the local food emporium does not count as exercise. Make sure that, whatever form you choose, you take regular exercise to keep both your mind and body in trim.

I know that exercise can be dull. However, it is also good *thinking time*. A period of running, walking or swimming means you can let your body do the work, leaving your mind free to deal with whatever is pressing on your thoughts that day. Think about joining a club or exercise class to help with your motivation if you need to.

There is a saying of *looking good, feeling good,* or is that just a marketing gimmick? Wherever the phrase originated, the two issues do go together. You may want to remember this after the fifth mile on the treadmill.

To demonstrate the benefits of exercise, the Mental Health Foundation maintains a report, entitled *Moving on up*, which focuses on the benefits of exercise as a way to treat depression. Further details are available from its website, which is *www.mentalhealth.org.uk*. Don't get me wrong: I am no saint, sitting here tapping away on my PC with an oversized belly, high blood pressure, a poor exercise regime and one too many glasses of wine last night. I also understand that writing does not count as exercise; if it did, I probably would not need a good exercise regime. But getting a regular medical check and watching your waistline are important for your own self esteem; they also help to make you attractive to others, if you are searching for new and exciting companionship.

You never know where Mr or Ms Right is going to show up and it's never when you expect them! Constant maintenance of all things 'you' is vital.

Your health

Personal health includes a multitude of categories. There are three areas you might want to consider. These are:

- General wellbeing

- Mental health

- Sexual health

As with anything medical, all the topics noted above are *specialist areas* and I am certainly not qualified to hand out advice on any of them. However, I have made some observations of studies, and considered some of the options available post-divorce that I hope will focus your mind on your own situation. I suggest that, if you are affected by any of these issues, you seek professional advice from your doctor or a specialist promptly to ensure that you are doing everything possible to look after yourself.

General wellbeing

I have already provided some notes on general wellbeing in this chapter and as a general observation, I understand that men tend to be more reluctant than women to seek medical advice. It might have been your ex-spouse who kept an eye on the family's health and because they have now gone, it is now solely down to you. So, make sure you take it seriously.

Health and wellbeing may not have been 'your department' in the previous marital unit. It may seem as alien to you as any other element of the household that was dealt with by your now ex-spouse. Be aware that they may be just as daunted at the prospect of managing money as you are about keeping yourself healthy, for example. The problem is that if they get it wrong, they may go overdrawn and get an expensive letter from the bank with the corresponding reprimand. If *you* get it wrong on the health front, you may not be around to see what the consequences are! Make sure that you put your health, both mental and physical, high on your agenda.

You should know that you are not alone. You can always refer to your doctor for help. If he or she cannot help you, they are likely to refer you to a specialist. For your mental health, you can again consult your doctor or you may choose to have some counselling to get you through a difficult period in your life. If you are fortunate enough to have Medical Insurance you may find that the provider will cover the cost of some consultations, but check the details first.

Counselling

Sometimes all you need is to talk things through in a secure, confidential and sympathetic environment, to make sense of what's happened, to understand why you feel the way you do, and to recognise your options in moving forward. This has the bonus of making sure that the burden you feel does not become overwhelming.

I have experienced counselling myself, and I found it highly beneficial. It made me realise better where I was in my recovery, post-divorce, and to understand my way forward. What's more, I feel no shame being a man admitting that I went to counselling. It didn't hurt, I was not embarrassed and it did help. As I learnt, coping with a situation does not have to be achieved alone.

Usually, you meet up with the same counsellor each week and pick up from your last session, gradually moving forward in a structured and focused environment. You can stop whenever you want and, as with most things in your life, you only get out of it what you are prepared to put in. If you are going to go along and not say much, then you are wasting your own time and money. However, if you feel you have a lot of burdens, then write the issues down below; prioritise them if you can, and think about why the points you have noted are important. This will allow you to get more out of your meetings. Additional space is also available at the 'Your notes' section at the end of this chapter.

Exercise

Tell me about the issues you want to cover through counselling?

_____

_____

What are your priorities?

_____

_____

Why is this important in your recovery?

_____

_____

You may want to show your counsellor your notes at the start of your programme.

Also remember that your counsellor, who is a trained and experienced professional, does not have a crystal ball. He or she can't put your world in order for you, and solve in one hour all of the issues you are facing. (If your counsellor does do this for you, give me their number please.) It is likely to take a few sessions, a handful maybe, to start to discover your own answers by doing not much more than merely discussing your circumstances, concerns and issues. Meetings are normally confidential and there may be a cost so you might want to check this before starting.

I used RELATE for my own counselling after divorce, although many other excellent organisations also offer this service.

Esther was referred to her counsellor by her doctor. The counsellor was a sole practitioner and not part of a group organisation. Nevertheless, highly recommended and very helpful. Your divorce solicitor may also have useful local contacts who may be able to help.

As already suggested, you don't need to cope alone with your changed circumstances. Counselling may be a way for someone you trust to 'hold your hand' as you make your transition to your new future.

Keep taking the pills!

Many of us are prescribed pills, potions and lotions for the ailments that we pick up on our travels through life. Whatever you do, if you are on prescribed medication, don't forget to keep up the course prescribed. This might be for a short period to solve an infection, or for longer lasting and even potentially permanent conditions, such as high blood pressure.

Keep your medication under control with the relevant doctor's checks, to ensure you keep yourself healthy. If you have to, keep a diary of when you need to replace your repeat prescription. Or you could store a reserve supply in a secure place to make sure you don't run out. Don't forget to re-stock this supply if you find yourself needing it.

If you are moving house, remember to update your address with your doctor and keep your pharmacist up to date. It is very easy to forget to place your prescription order in the turmoil of the divorce recovery change, and soon find yourself running out of the potions that keep you ticking.

Mental health

According to the Mental Health Foundation, based on research from other organisations, such as The Office for National Statistics' report, *Psychiatric Morbidity in Great Britain*, various statistics are available about mental health:

- 1 in 4 people will experience some kind of mental health problem in the course of a year

- Depression and mixed anxiety is the most common mental disorder in Britain

- Depression affects 1 in 5 older people living in the community

Further details of the Mental Health Foundation's work and additional statistics can be found at their website, *www.mentalhealth.org.uk.*

If you are beginning to struggle with your own wellbeing — or with your menatl stability — then do seek advice from your doctor as soon as possible. Talk to close friends or family and ask for their support in guiding you through this period in your life.

Many specialist support organisations for mental health, both locally and nationally, can help you. I have listed a few of these below, with their website addresses:

Mind — *www.mind.org.uk*

Mental Health Foundation — *www.mentalhealth.org.uk*

Relate — *www.relate.org.uk*

Whatever you do, make sure that you identify any issues as soon as you can and seek qualified help.

Sexual health

Having looked at general wellbeing and mental health, this part of the chapter we will consider some of the issues surrounding sexual health. However, this usually starts with moving on in your life with a new partner or the dating game.

The gift of time

You are still the same wonderful individual you were before your ex-spouse possibly dragged you through the divorce courts and made you out to be the villain of the piece. Now that you are officially single again, it may not be long before you attract the attentions of another suitor, so you may need to be prepared for this.

When preparing my thoughts for this section, I thought about age ranges and whether this would affect the points to be made about finding new companionship, love and intimacy — if indeed that's what you are keen to achieve. It makes little difference what age you are when you divorce and start again, whether you are twenty-five or over sixty-five. You might be a bit friskier the younger you are, but emotionally, many of us never leave our twenties. Only our bodies really get older.

Age does not feature as an issue here because happiness, fulfilment and love are not bound by time or age. If your divorce happened when the children had left for university at eighteen (you might be around fifty years old) then you would typically have approximately thirty to thirty-five years of life to enjoy yourself, with or without a new partner. That's a long time and you can fit a lot into three decades. Go for it!

If you do feel restricted by your age, then I have to tell you that this feeling is self-inflicted. You may not feel like doing a bungee jump or a sky dive this week, but that does not mean you shouldn't have a fun and a highly active existence. This may be on your own or with a partner, and if it's with a partner, then you will have to start dating again.

Dating again?

The dating game is not easy for most people. There are lots of people out there, back on the circuit and ready to start living again. Just like you, they find themselves back *in the game*, wondering what to do next. It's important to figure out what is your motivation (and not just lust) — and possibly even more importantly, what is *their* motivation — for dating again. Are you looking for companionship, love, sex, a stable financial future, or something else?

The question above may seem a little blunt. However, these questions need to be asked of both you *and* any new companion that comes along. (But it's not recommended as an ice-breaker on the first date.) That's why I have headed this section *the gift of time*. You may need time to understand what you want from the future, and this might mean some self-contemplation. It also might mean playing the field a bit, to remind yourself of what your options are and what kind of people you want to be with.

To back up this point, I have spoken to many a divorce solicitor who feels that they have been doing the job for too long, because of clients who return to them for a divorce for the second or third time in the last ten to fifteen years.

Unfortunately, the statistics for the failure of second and third marriages in the UK speak for themselves. Bear this in mind and don't rush into anything (source: www.statistics.gov.uk).

This will sound a very selfish thing to consider, but what would a new marriage do for you? What's in it for you? Mercenary or not, someone should be asking you this hard question. If no one else has, then it might as well be me. You might think this is a bit *rich* coming from me with my track record. I wish someone had done this for me.

Remember what we said earlier about personal standards; does any new suitor meet your standards, or are you making do? If you should find yourself on the point of re-marrying, ask yourself *why?* I hope that you get a full and convincing answer.

Even more importantly, ask exactly the same question of your new partner and proposed fiancée. I hope you know them well enough by now to know what they are really saying.

What's the rush?

My message when looking at any new relationship is *please take your time*. There is a very wise saying: *'Marry in haste, repent at leisure!'* You are in no hurry.

Even when you do meet a suitable partner, there is no need to rush into a new marriage until both of you are ready. It is worth allowing a while for the effects of the previous divorce to sink in, and to learn the lessons from what went wrong last time, before moving on to the next and hopefully final union in your life.

There is a risk in running relationships into one another. Hopping from one marriage straight into another relationship may mean that you forget or fail to acknowledge any issues that may need resolving. The worst that could happen is that you remarry quickly and then find yourself divorced again over exactly the same issues.

Pausing to take stock may not feel the most natural thing to do, especially when you are all 'loved up' in the whirlwind of your new relationship. However, it will give you a chance to contemplate two important things.

Firstly, what you have learned from the past?

Secondly, and more importantly, what do you want from the future?

Only the passage of time will allow you to know what's best for you.

Taking time for this may not suit your new partner's ambitions. However, if they love you, they should understand your need for a neutral period before committing again. There is no hurry to remarry and if there is, pause to ask yourself *why?* Is this a case of you rushing your choice, or is it pressure coming from someone else? You might have a fair reason for pushing ahead so quickly — but is that reason in itself enough to justify a new marriage at this stage in your life?

It's not hard to remember how painful the last divorce was, and you don't want to go through that again, do you? Although you may be getting swept along with the arranging of a wedding, remember the cancellation costs are far cheaper than another divorce!

Still not convinced? A study by Professor Ted Huston, (Professor of Human Ecology at the University of Texas, was recently published in the US Journal, *Personal Relationships,* might be worth reading.

The researchers studied 168 couples over fourteen years. One of the most startling conclusions was that the seeds of divorce could often be detected right at the start of the relationship. He found that those couples with the shortest courtship were more likely to split up than those that took extended periods of time together before marrying. He adds: 'Positive feelings, such as trust and respect, emerge and the whole thing mirrors the evolution of any other kind of good relationship in life.'

'Best friend' relationships tended to be the most successful. And by their very nature, they take a long time to develop.

Getting it wrong can happen in many ways, and it can manifest itself in a more physical form than the simple fact of a divorce. The growth in sexually transmitted diseases and HIV in the over-fifties has been significant in recent years. Some might put this incarnation down to the invention of a trapezoidal blue pill that keeps parts of a male's body going for longer than would normally be natural.

Sexually transmitted diseases are not just for the young

It would not be wise to talk about dating, new liaisons and sexual encounters without bringing up the subject of sexually transmitted diseases, or STDs for short.

Reported sexually transmitted diseases, from Syphilis and Chlamydia, through to HIV (AIDS), continues to grow in the age groups 45-64 and the over-65s. As an example, according to the Health Protection Agency, Gonorrhoea saw an 11 per cent increase in the over 65's between 2002 and 2006.

Taking this further, a study published in July 2010 in *AIDS (Sexually Transmitted Diseases (STDs) Health Protection Agency Research. Published in the Journal, AIDS, July 2010)* suggests that 'half of older adults diagnosed during the study period [2000-2007] were infected at age 50 or over' in England, Wales and Northern Ireland. In addition, the study found that the number of over-50s seeking treatment for HIV in the UK had shown a *significant increase*, rising threefold during the study period. The research did note that this was partly because of increased survival rates, as well as the number of people diagnosed soon after infection at age 50 or more. *(Source: Health Protection Agency: Centre for Infections Research)*

These statistics are pretty stark and indicate something that may never occur to a newly divorced and now dating or involved individual. You might have thought about these things in your youth, but not now. An STD is the last thing you need at this point in your recovery from the trial of your divorce.

It maybe too easy to forget protection or to think that life is too short and now is the time to enjoy yourself, and I would not want to stop you doing this. However, just remember, as you did when you were dating the first time around, to take the appropriate precautions. I won't tell you how to run your life and especially your new sex life, but you are more mature now than you were all those years ago. You can apply a bit of common sense to the situations you are encountering, backed up by the implications of the various academic studies noted previously.

Recognising the long term detrimental effects in the UK, the sexual health charity, FPA (formerly the Family Planning Association) has targeted 'baby boomers' (those born between 1945 and around 1960) in a national campaign called Sexual Health Week to persuade the over-fifties to practise safe sex.

Their website is *www.fpa.org.uk.*

As ever, the straightforward advice is *always wear a condom!*

Just to drive home the message about the risks you run in not protecting yourself, here are a few additional and quite daunting facts:

In the UK, it is possible for the full development of late stage HIV or AIDS to take around 10 years from infection to materialise. Sometimes HIV shows few symptoms (source: Terence Higgins Trust Website, www.tht.org.uk).

This is not happy reading, I appreciate. However, you do not want ignorance to be your biggest enemy. If you are concerned by any of these issues then visit your doctor or Health Centre for help and advice.

Over to you now

No one should tell you how to run your life and I am not doing that in this chapter or book. You will do what you want to anyway, irrespective of your age, sex or circumstances.

The release from a marriage may give you new confidence to experiment and do things you have never tried before and with new and exciting people. It sounds like great fun and I hope it is. I trust that you have many, many years ahead of you to have a good time. Looking after yourself now will pay dividends in those latter times.

In summary, before you rush off to do all of the things that everyone told you not to do, take a moment to think about the consequences for your health.

Don't do it for me, but for you and your own future.

Your Notes

What health issues, if any, are affecting you and what are you planning to do to correct this?

What programme or checklist will you use to monitor your health into the future?

Nagged, Tagged and Bagged...

Chapter Six

The process of change

Wouldn't it be useful to have a TARDIS at this point in your life? It could ship you off effortlessly to a new and very different destination, preferably while no one else, like Doctor Who, was using it. You could pop inside, pour yourself a drink, polish the Dalek memorabilia collection, find a hole to stick your sonic screwdriver into and then punch in some coordinates to the future and a place that you wanted to be. As with the fictional character, these actions would usually be because you were hurrying away from a heap of trouble that has your name on it and is about to squash you forever. Does this sound familiar at all?

Sadly, TARDISes are in short supply to everyone but Time Lords. In your *divorce recovery*, you know that change is going to have to occur — and these changes may affect every aspect of your life.

The very nature of being separated, divorced or even bereaved means that you are going to face the future on your own or with someone new. However, *change* is not a swear word. Change should be embraced, even nurtured, however reluctant you may feel at first. But there has to be a *desire* to change, a *conviction* in your innermost self that it's time for a difference in your life.

A personal view of change

To change is to be creative and many people resist this. I have chosen some of my favourite quotations to provide a flavour of what has been considered from the past and what you might want to consider whilst looking at your own change process:

'To improve is to change. To be perfect is to change often.' — *Winston Churchill*

'Progress is a nice word. But change is its motivator and change has its enemies.' — *Robert Kennedy*

'Change is not merely necessary to life — it is life.' — *Alvin Toffler*

And the final one, whose irony made me laugh, is:

'Change is like putting lipstick on a bulldog. The bulldog's appearance has not improved, but now it's really angry.' — *Rosbeth Moss Kanter*

I am sure that some people in this new change situation feel like a lipsticked bulldog sometimes. They may be very angry about a change that has been forced upon them by some lipstick-wielding past 'owner' who has daubed them up as a divorcee and then stood back to sneer at their handiwork.

Like the bulldog above, you must wash off such undeserved marking and continue on your way.

Means and motivation

What is your motivation for change? What is your target? If you don't have one yet, think about what it would be. Like most decisions in life, there usually have to be two prevailing factors to make change happen. One is *means*, the money, energy or time to make a change happen. An example might be the ability to afford a house move or qualifications for a new job.

The other is *motivation*, a desire to go from where you are to where, or what, you want to be. Think about something you have already achieved in the past that made a really positive change in your life. It might have been passing an exam, giving up smoking, starting a business, getting married or making sure you gave your kids a good education. These are the tasks you undertook to get your change to occur.

But *what* is the motivation? To know that, you need to know what your target is. Let's look at your examples again. Passing an exam might have got you the job you wanted, which got you a higher salary, which led you to a better lifestyle. Giving up smoking probably made you feel better and will allow you to live longer, giving you more time to enjoy yourself with friends and family.

What is your motivation and target? Use the next exercise to detail your objectives.

Exercise

What is your motivation / motivator?

_____

_____

_____

What do you want to achieve into the future?

_____

_____

_____

Why is this your target?

_____

_____

_____

Extra notes space has been made available at the end of this chapter.

Do you see how this works? The change you make is nothing more than the conduit to the desired effect on your future. Change is the *delivery* of the motivation of what you want to achieve.

The change that you choose does not have to be large. Just a tweak to your normal routine, on its own — or it might be a combination of minor changes — may make all the difference to how soon you reach your goal or goals.

Your personal goal could be and are often purely selfish. It might be fuelled by love, greed, fear or even status. It's almost always a question of *what's in it for me?*

This can be extended to family as well; pushing the kids through school, for example, to get good exam passes. The benefit to *you* in doing this might be that they no longer become an emotional or financial drain on you in later life, or still be living with you at the age of thirty. As suggested in na earlier chapter, the life changes that are experienced by children are significant and usually experienced at a far quicker pace than those that happen in adult life.

Communicating change to others

To get the best for your children, or anyone else for that matter, may depend on the way that we communicate with them.

When you hear someone say: '*I've told you a hundred times before . . .*' about anything, it always sounds like a parent or employer chastising a child or staff member for some misdemeanour. Think about the saying though. If no one is listening or the recipient does not understand the message being given, who is at fault? It is always the person delivering the message, no matter how many times they repeat it.

If there is no reason for the listener to 'buy in' to the message of change, nothing positive will happen. The only results will be frustration and irritation. You don't want to run your life on those lines, do you?

At this stage it must be remembered that your ex-spouse or former partner may have also been your best friend and, intentionally or not, the decision maker. You may have relied on him or her for years to do what's best for the household. Many relationships work this way, with lines of responsibility being drawn over time. One person does the family finances, the other the shopping and ironing, with both taking joint responsibility of the summer holiday or the children's homework.

Following the separation, those lines are removed. You may find yourself considering issues in an area that you know little about, having surrendered your knowledge of such topics to another party decades ago. You have a steep learning curve to climb, but climb it you must. Are you ready for your transformation?

I talked about 'buy in' earlier. Along with others, you need to buy into your own change programme to get the best from your future. Of course, there will be a degree of risk involved — but this risk is coupled with an opportunity for self-discovery. Change is not going to work if you don't buy into it. Any change for the better involves going through a process.

The factors that you need to add into your personal change programme are unique to you. Everyone is different. However, these variations tend to follow a similar cycle or pattern and I have detailed the process of change in the next section. This may mean that you undertake many changes from this point onwards, using a similar decision making process for tangible and intangible items.

Deciding what to change when

So, you are going to make a few changes in your life. Have you written them down and put them into priority order? One change may not be achievable without another happening first.

Exercise

List your planned changes here:

_____

_____

_____

_____

'What's your priority order?':

_____

_____

_____

_____

Extra notes space has been made available at the end of this chapter.

You should think about the sequence of your life changes before setting the ball rolling. Would one change be better delayed to allow the first change to take its full effect? Plan your priorities carefully to get the best outcome.

These are the factors for change you should be thinking about now:

Attention: to the need to change and why you want to

Interest: in understanding why you want to change. *What's in it for you?*

Conviction: that the change chosen is in your best interests

Desire: that the target of your aspirations is what you really want for your future

Change: how you will actually deliver your change

You may alter the key words above to suit your own style or situation. However, I'm sure you have got the message: not just *what* you need to do, but most importantly *why* you need to identify the reasons for this renewal of *you* to happen.

Without wishing to cheapen this idea, the change process is similar to a standard buying process for a physical item. The change process for emotion is, by its nature, intangible; this is why it is worth having a process to understand *why* you are making your journey of discovery.

When was the last time you made a purchase of a large consumable item, such as a car or kitchen? As an example, when you buy a car, you will normally go through a buying process of Attention, Interest, Conviction, Desire —— and the closure of the deal (Change) by driving away the car that you coveted.

In this process, your **attention** might involve viewing the car online or ordering a brochure.

Your **interest** might be visiting a showroom to look at a car.

Conviction might be to touch the car or sit in it.

Desire might be a test drive and negotiating the final price.

Finally, you part with your hard earned cash and drive away, having made the **change** of car and closed the deal.

Any good car salesman will tell you they never approach a prospective buyer in a showroom until the buyer has physically touched the car. This is because the potential buyer is going through the process of identifying what they wants to purchase and getting sufficient conviction about it to touch and sit in the vehicle.

If you learn nothing else from this section, you can now identify your weak point when in a car showroom.

Returning to the more important vehicle, *yourself* in the divorce process, you have either 'traded-in' or 'been traded-in', like an older car. Now it's time to buy into another model to match your new anticipated lifestyle.

Returning to our stages of Attention, Interest, Conviction, Desire and Change, here are some more emotive thoughts:

Attention

Attention to detail is the first point. Who is looking after you? Are you making the best of what you yourself have to offer, assuming you do want to offer and attract the right sort of partner for the future? This may mean going through a process of acceptance that you might *not* be doing the best for yourself, avoiding any points of denial that everything is fine, when it clearly isn't. This in turn may bring you through a period of annoyance, even anger, knowing that you might have let yourself down a bit. Had you paid a bit more attention to 'you' in the first place, this whole situation might have been avoided?

Interest

Do you know where you are going and how you want to change? You must be *interested* in knowing what your journey of change is going to look like, which location you want this chosen change to occur in, and possibly how quickly you want the chosen change to occur. No one is going to be as interested in 'you' as *you* are. Some of these factors will be outside your control, but thinking forward will clarify your interest in how the future could look. You also need to pick the *target* of the change that you will eventually desire. This could be a person, a job, a home or relocation. You know better than anyone else what your personal target is; it's now a question of how you achieve it.

Conviction

Conviction is how you understand that you will never get where you want to be without some effort, interest (even sacrifice) and attention to detail, based on the objective of your chosen target. If your heart isn't in the change process, you are unlikely to be motivated to meet your target the way you want to.

This might mean that you fall short of what you want to achieve, and this in turn could throw your true desire into question.

You need to focus on your conviction to achieve your target. Looking back at your past self, you may now find yourself crossing personal boundaries you would never have considered before. On reflection, this opens up a whole new world of possibilities. Stepping outside your comfort zone is never easy; do you have the conviction you will need? Go for it!

Desire

You have identified the target, you have the conviction that it's the right target and you desire its virtues. It has interested you for a while and the desire hasn't waned. As if you were the car for sale, having polished yourself up in your intention to gain attention, you have viewed the target buyer, possibly gone for a test drive, and let them know you are interested in a negotiation so you can drive into the sunset together.

Joking aside, you will need to do all of these things to get the desired result, overcoming a few obstacles in the process; if you have gone this far, you will be sure that whatever you are focused on *is* the right target.

Finally, the change itself (Closing your deal)

The truth is that if you have been working on the *factors for change* above, change will come to you naturally and you may be close to achieving what motivated you in the first place.

I talked earlier about embracing change. However, it is the other factors that you must embrace and change will naturally follow; both in terms of what you wanted to change, and, with this new learning, possibly also your view on what can be achieved in other areas of your life when you focus. You are only limited by your own imagination.

The world is there to be changed and change is a good thing, although it involves energy and motivation from you. I cannot help you further with your motivations or desires, because only you can know what you want to do and why. The change process I've outlined will help you with identifying where you are in making those motivations and desires real.

By reading this chapter and the other thoughts in this book, I hope you are already on your way to understanding a way towards your new, improved future.

Don't just think it — write it down

You may have taken some time to fathom out what you want from your future. It's a complicated subject and you will need to map out the way ahead. Some people head straight for the target; others don't.

Whichever camp you find yourself in at the beginning, I strongly suggest that you write down how you see it working out for you. This can be in a notepad, the space below, or on your computer, wherever you prefer. Just get the information down in writing somewhere so that you can refer to it on a regular basis. This will allow you to add to your initial thoughts, scrub out bits that didn't work, and adjust your findings as your understanding develops.

Exercise

What do you want from the future?

_____

_____

_____

What's your main target and why?

_____

_____

_____

_____

Extra notes space has been made available at the end of this chapter.

I once got so confused by an emotional situation that I got out a roll of wallpaper and put it on the dining room floor, upside down on the blank side, secured each end with stones, and then drew out my planned progress with a black marker pen. At about twelve feet long I could actually walk along my intended progress, looking backwards and forwards to see errors or improvements that could be added or subtracted.

It was a great exercise. Whenever I got stuck after that, I could roll out the wallpaper and see where I was up to. If I had more to add, I just kept rolling out another five feet of wallpaper and scrawled away. If it was warm and dry outside, I could lay the wallpaper out in the garden and work on my plans there.

Try it! I highly recommend this very cheap option . . . but make sure the marker pen does not go through to the carpet (as mine did!).

Having considered entering a process of change — and it should be noted that there are several alternatives to choose from — and armed with your new positive attitude focused on what you really want to achieve, your personal TARDIS should begin to take shape and direction, allowing you to make the significant changes that you want. You are to become your own Time Lord.

The concept of moving yourself around mentally and physically from one place to another is of course completely different to that of a fictional time-travelling Police telephone box TARDIS. However, the rest of the image of moving and changing into something different and achievable is perfectly real.

It's down to you to make it happen.

Your Notes

What are you going to change for your future and why is this important to you?

What timeframe are you anticipating this change process will take?

How do you plan to reward yourself when the change you desire is complete?

Nagged, Tagged and Bagged...

Chapter Seven

Money matters

Money. Where do you start with this subject? And possibly even more importantly, where do you end with money?

The Little Oxford Dictionary defines Money as: *Current Coin; Bank notes or other documents representing it; wealth.* Is it money itself that we are interested in or more the *wealth* angle we aspire to? Are they both the same thing?

The definition of wealth is: *Riches; being rich; abundance, a profusion of.* You can have a wealth of anything, from knowledge to money to (hopefully) health. You may be less interested in a 'wealth of knowledge' right now, as this won't pay the mortgage or the gas bill; like the Chancellor of the Exchequer, you want to bring the threads of your economy together.

I have spent nearly all my working life planning money: arranging the lending of it, the banking of it and coming up with strategies for making it work harder and for longer. Like water, money flows through an economy, whether that economy is a global one or just your personal bank account. Without care, money can also be as uncontrollable as water.

Security and planning

Planning your new future is also going to involve planning your money, both in the immediate weekly shopping basket and in the longer term for things like housing, holidays and retirement.

This will mean a bit of financial planning and personal budgeting to make the ends of your possibly threadbare income meet — or at least to know how much of an abyss your finances have fallen into. At least knowing all this will show you how far you need to travel, to get back to your intended starting point and beyond.

Make sure you take charge of your savings and banking quickly, and that these are held in your sole name. Get yourself a shredder and get rid of any unrequired paperwork you may have accumulated that you no longer need. Make sure that you keep your records and statements for banking and tax, as examples. Put any important documents that you do need to keep in a safe and secure place and this might include your passport, will, policy documents, birth certificate and so on. Many home safes are both cheap and easy to install, so it might be worth thinking about getting one.

If you do not understand —or do not want to understand — all things financial, then make sure you take advice from someone who does. This might be a well-versed and trusted relative, friend, independent financial adviser or an accountant, for example.

Make sure you keep an eye on any debts that you may have accumulated and keep the repayment of this debt serviced to ensure that it does not get out of control. You would not want your credit rating to take a dive when you are just about to try and buy a new home and get a mortgage. If you are struggling to meet your liabilities, then talk to your lending institutions or speak to the Citizens Advice Bureau about how to control the situation. Their website address is *www.citizensadvice.org.uk.*

At this point, I could probably list out a whole raft of notes about what you should think about when dealing with your finances and the various parts of the interconnected planning you should administer. This is beyond the scope of this book, although there are some points that I believe are relevant to the issue of recovery, especially after a divorce, and I have included them. They are not in any specific order and it should be noted that this is not an exhaustive list.

If you feel that you need additional financial guidance or administration —— and that unwieldy feeling of not knowing what's happening should give you a clue— then speak to an independent financial adviser who is qualified to help you move your finances forward. Ask for a recommendation from someone you trust; they should be able to guide you to someone locally.

Here we go then. Financials and all things administration, in a nutshell:

Passport

At the back of your passport on the last page, you should normally detail whom you want to be contacted in the event of an emergency in a foreign land. Many people miss this. If you are planning a post-divorce break abroad, whether or not it's a celebration, you might want to review this page and amend the contact details if required.

You may not want them calling your ex-spouse after an accident whilst you're having a frisky weekend away with a new partner.

Pension

If you have pension benefits, and most people do, you may have been able to make a nomination for these benefits in the event of your death before retirement. Now that you are divorced, you may want to change that nomination to someone else, unless you agreed not to in your financial settlement. This might include your children, parents or your new partner. As you life settles down, you can change this again to meet your new circumstances as they evolve.

The proceeds of the pension fund before drawing benefits should fall outside your estate for inheritance tax purposes, and are usually paid quite quickly, otherwise this may go to your estate. If you have an employer's benefit arrangement, such as a death in service scheme and pension rights, you may want to discuss this nomination with your Human Resources department and update your wishes according to your new circumstances.

Pension sharing orders

If you were the recepient of a pension sharing order then you will have to organise where these funds are to be held for your future. Ideally, the pension order needs to be dealt with promptly after the *Decree Absolute* is finalised. You may want to speak to an independent financial adviser about what is best for you and the new benefits available to you.

Perhaps you were on the other end of the transaction, giving the pension funds away? In that case, you might wish to revisit your pension planning strategy as it is likely to have changed, in some cases significantly. You might have planned to retire at age 60 with a comfortable income of so-many thousand pounds per annum to enjoy in your twilight years. Now that the pension share order is in place, both the age and amount available to you may have evaporated and you might want to look again at what any new projections hold for you.

Some people prefer just not to look, as the bright picture of a happy retirement may have turned into *a postcard from poverty.*

Insurance and investment plans

Make sure you update your insurance, investment and pension providers with your new home address to ensure that any correspondence does not go to the old matrimonial home. This includes any children's policies, savings plans or deposit accounts that you hold for them until they reach majority.

I am sure that you don't want your personal information getting into the wrong hands.

State pension forecast

Post-divorce, you may find that your state pension benefits may change. You can check this by completing a new state pension forecast (Form BR19) with your new details, including the date of your divorce. Send this to the Pensions Service, at the Department of Work and Pensions in Newcastle. They will normally take about three to six weeks to update this information for you.

You should note, however, that this forecast may again change if you re-marry.

Update your will

I firmly believe that everyone who reaches the age of majority should write a will. Talk to your legal advisers or solicitors about sorting out this document and store it safely thereafter.

Many solicitors offering matrimonial services can also provide will services. It may be easiest to get an introduction to an appropriate professional this way. If your personal budget is tight — and after a divorce this may be likely — then many stationers offer 'Will Kits', a cheap and convenient alternative, even if it is only a short term measure. In my opinion, it is better to have a cheap and simple will than no will at all, but read the instructions carefully.

When you have made a will, keep it safe and let someone you trust know where it is, to ensure that your wishes are followed if you die.

Finally, be wary about the offer of 'free will' services. If it looks too good to be true, it usually is. The organisations that offer *free* wills are usually not charities; they are likely to make their money in the future when you die, charging a percentage value on your estate to administer the arrangement. This can mean that your children and loved ones find themselves paying a hefty bill when you are gone.

As ever, always read the small print.

Re-negotiating maintenance agreements

As we move through this time of austerity, changes in maintenance payments may come to mind, especially in the event of issues such as a loss of a job, which then means that the agreed payment becomes unaffordable.

As part of your financial settlement, you may have agreed to a maintenance payment level on an ongoing basis, say monthly, in better economic times. Maintenance payments can be varied or terminated. Sometimes this is because there is a change in circumstance, such as loss of employment and on other occasions because a specific event has occurred, such as cohabitation or remarriage, or your children reaching eighteen.

Couples who have a court order, or separation agreement in place dealing with maintenance, will need to be guided by the terms of their order or agreement, which may make it clear the events that will cause maintenance to change, or stop all together. If they then agree on a new amount, the new arrangements can be formally approved through your solicitors and the court. If the order or agreement is *silent* as to when maintenance might change or stop, either party can still seek a variation of the maintenance payments when there is a change in circumstance and can apply to the court to consider this, if they and their former spouse cannot reach agreement.

Those couples, who have resolved matters between themselves and have no formal court order or separation agreement, can renegotiate terms at any time.

Of course, being pragmatic about the situation and negotiation, particularly in difficult economic times, should be a sensible approach. For couples who cannot agree on a way forward mediation may be helpful and cost effective.

As an additional note, maintenance payments made by you to your former spouse cease automatically by operation of the current law, if your former spouse remarries. The payments do not however stop when the paying party remarries.

Taking the note above further, if his or her relationship develops, don't expect to be at the top of the guest list for the marriage of your ex-spouse and their new intended. This is not surprising of course. However, it is not impossible for someone to forget to advise their ex-spouse that they are remarried, meaning that the maintenance payments could stop. You might wish to monitor this situation if you feel that this type of change may occur.

If you are in this position or uncertain on your position, then take good legal advice as soon as possible.

There are usually two reasons why maintenance may change. Let me explain.

Original maintenance agreement

Some negotiations might be prompted by a clause in the original agreement, such as a cohabitation, which confirms that in the event of this occurring, the previous spouse no longer has to pay at the agreed maintenance level.

If your former spouse starts to live with another person this may not automatically trigger a reduction in your maintenance payments to her, you need to look at the terms of your divorce or separation agreement. If you have not negotiated that cohabitation will automatically cause a reduction in the maintenance payments, you can still seek a variation at the time because of the change in circumstance. The court will however look at the situation on its merits at the time. Cohabitation is not necessarily an automatic reason for maintenance to cease, particularly when you still have dependent children living with your former spouse. It may be a reason however for maintenance to be reduced.

Maintenance can be paid at what is called a 'nominal' amount, usually 5p or £1 a year. This is to keep open a former spouse's claims against the other spouse's income. The recipient of a nominal order can apply during the term of the maintenance payment to increase it to a more substantial amount if there is a change in circumstance. It is also possible for maintenance to be reduced to a nominal level, rather than for it to be extinguished, for example, where a former spouse is cohabiting but has not remarried. This then means that were the cohabitation to be unsuccessful the former spouse can seek for the nominal maintenance to be increased to a higher level again.

In addition, most maintenance agreements are time-bound. This may mean that they are payable only until the previous spouse reaches a pre-defined age, such as retirement, or when a child leaves full-time education. Some agreements are not time-bound, and these would have been negotiated at the time of the divorce, although, as an example, these are more common for those involved in long marriages.

If you are unsure of your situation, you may decide to revisit your *Financial Settlement* to confirm to yourself when the need for maintenance to be paid ends. This is just as important for the payer to know as it is for the receiver.

Debt control

In the process of getting divorced you may have accrued some debts in order to make ends meet. These will need to be kept under control or repaid to keep any interest costs to a minimum.

You may have outstanding solicitor's costs, credit card debts and bank account overdrafts to contend with. The relentless monotony of how the reminders for all these arrive within quick succession of each other will certainly test your inner strength. You will also know that the rates of interest charged by credit cards are usually high and need to be monitored.

Where you have received a payment as part of your settlement, you should consider the advantages of clearing any debts you may have as soon as possible. This decision needs to take into consideration any need you have to maintain an emergency fund of savings to protect yourself against unforeseen circumstances.

Assuming you don't have sufficient cash to pay off your debts, then consider whom you owe what, the timescale of your requirement to repay, and also the cost of delaying repayment – all good planning techniques.

For example, a solicitor's bill may only give you thirty days to pay and this may not be negotiable. On the other hand, a credit card may not need to be repaid straight away, but as you know, the provider will usually charge you handsomely for the privilege of delaying settlement, increasing the overall cost. If you are expecting a settlement payment from your divorce, then make sure that you know when this will arrive in your bank account and how much it will be.

Whilst you are balancing your budget at this point, it is worth checking and comparing the interest charges on any loan or credit card to see if interest savings can be achieved with another provider. Many comparison sites can make this easier — but as with all things financial, carefully read the small print, and any terms and conditions, to make sure you don't get caught out by expensive clauses or additional charges.

However you deal with this financial balancing situation, the one thing you must not do is ignore debt. Communication is the key to a successful transition away from debt with your lenders. Debt won't go away and you don't want to miss payments and ruin your credit rating at this stage in your divorce recovery. Should you find yourself stuck or struggling, seek some financial advice from a trusted adviser. Again, as an alternative, the Citizens Advice Bureau may be able to point you in the right direction.

Prenuptial (Pre-Nups) agreements

Pre-Nups: In my opinion, the very definition of a passion killer.

A prenuptial agreement is a legal document incorporating a financial agreement between two parties prior to a marriage, to confirm who is entitled to what, should the union falter in the future.

Prevalent in the United States, they have not been widely used in England and Wales. In America, some agreements are time-bound — and there have been some high profile cases of the divorce proceedings being issued, coincidentally, just before the end of the agreement is due to fall.

These have been binding in America for some time and have been widely publicised for celebrities and the like. The situation in England and Wales is now changing. The first high profile case of *Radmacher (the Supreme Court ruling 2010)* confirmed that, although they are not currently binding, the court should give effect to these types of agreement if entered into freely with full understanding, unless it is thought unfair, to hold the parties to the agreement. This is a highly topical and changing area and much text will follow in the years to come, therefore take good advice if you need to consider this option.

Prenuptial agreements may have their benefits. They make it clear at the outset 'who gets what' with a view to ensuring that there is no ambiguity in the event of the parties separating. However, some people prefer to assume that love conquers all, and that if you can't trust your partner at the outset, you should not enter the union in the first place.

There is no obligation to have one in place, and this option is voluntary.

Divorce insurance and Pre-Nups . . . the future?

Whilst writing this book, my knowledge of a new concept of 'Divorce Insurance' came to the fore. With the advantages of Legal Aid being withdrawn from divorce cases due to the austerity cuts, the suggestion of *divorce insurance* has been born in the UK, although I understand that this purchasable protection has been available in America since 2005 (source: Daily Mail). With this concept and that of prenuptial agreements (also now gaining legal traction in England and Wales), the possibility of securing yourself financially before entering into a marriage union seems close at hand. This idea will clearly have its critics who would argue that this goes against the trust that marriage should instil in a relationship, however, I doubt that commercial organisations will allow that to get in their way. Clearly, divorce is an expensive business and the ending of Legal Aid for divorcing couples and family disputes is suggested to save £178 million a year. I am sure the devil will be in the detail of these plans as competitors come to the market.

Jam tomorrow

The viability of 'a life of milk and honey' may have gone since the divorce. The reality of the financial settlement that you agreed to in the heat of the legal battle may only now be hitting home as you settle into the routine of a new life, either as a single person or with the party that may have been the cause of the divorce in the first place.

The money side of things does require some speedy and focused attention, and it has to be balanced with your emotions.

On the one hand, you may want to go out every night to celebrate your new found single life, almost like a teenager, but with a lot more money to lose. On the other, you may be paying maintenance whilst also trying to manage a new home, either owned or rented, and also trying to put your life back on track.

The adoption of the *spend what you can't afford now and worry about tomorrow, tomorrow* attitude may well be a foolhardy approach, but it's not uncommon. I see it so often after a divorce and, in a way, this is only natural. In the euphoria or sadness of being newly divorced, it is easy to forget that you need to pay for such things as mortgages, school uniforms and children's presents.

Some people prefer, in the early weeks, to spend what seems like surplus funds on social frippery and entertaining. I am not being Mr Miserable here, and I know we all need to live again and let our hair down.

The smart thing is to find the right balance between being responsible for whoever relies on you, or pays you maintenance; and being like an uncaged bird, flying as free and high as you can. Overspending in your recovery stage will more than likely come back to bite you sooner or later. Finding that balance early is worthwhile.

Budget planning

One easy way to consider your budget is to list out the **assets**, **income**, **liabilities** and **outgoings** for which you are now responsible, and tally these up to see whether you're in surplus or deficit.

Many people find it easier to do this in a prescribed format, and you may want to use a spreadsheet modeller as an example. You can find these on the Internet; some good and cost effective examples I can think of are www.moneydashboard.com or www.budgettracker.com. Microsoft also offers a budget spreadsheet download facility which might meet your needs.

Other people prefer to do this on paper and the exercise overleaf may help.

Exercise

Consider listing out your;

Assets

Income

Liabilities

Outgoings

Extra notes space has been made available at the end of this chapter.

You may have had to complete a *Form E* before your divorce and Financial Settlement. Many of us would prefer to forget it, but that was a useful source of information on what you had, what you brought in and what your outgoings were. As unattractive as it is to revisit that previous court submission, the form itself does focus the mind on what needs to be considered.

To find a fresh form, visit Her Majesty's Courts Service website at *www.hmcs.gov.uk* and download a sample which you can now complete with the fresh information to reflect your post-divorce circumstances.

The one key point in undertaking this personal exercise is to be honest with yourself. Put in the true *pluses* and *minuses*. Many divorced clients come to see me to work through this planning together, considering incomes and outgoings, likely pension benefits and tax free cash, challenging their own financial thinking and direction to ensure that it is a robust model that won't lead them into trouble.

It's always great news if it turns out that there are surpluses that can be spent on new partners, or sports cars or motorcycles to enable the driver (usually male) to deny their true age. (His ability to dismount that motorcycle with any panache at all will usually give away his true level of maturity.)

It is crucial to catch any deficits early and to cut the household outgoings where possible so that finances are kept under control. I remember at one point, I was checking *my* personal finances on a daily basis. For some people, this remains a daily routine, however at the time I thought it a bit extreme and cut down to checking around once a week.

In hindsight, I can confirm that a regular and thorough check is usually worthwhile; it's almost a damage limitation exercise. This does not mean that you will never live the high life again, never go on holiday again, or never prosper into an affluent lifestyle in the future; it just means that your progress through your life changes will need to be planned carefully, rather than just happen without due attention to your day-to-day financial condition.

It's all very well thinking about what money you had — but that is historic. What matters now is what you plan to do with your current income and assets and how you deploy your possibly greatly reduced assets.

Do something that scares you!

After my own divorce, I decided that starting a company was the way forward, and then was the time to do it. With a lot of help from Esther, my wife, in various ways (such as financial, emotional, business knowledge) the business started with relatively meagre funds and has traded successfully ever since. This was a great challenge at that particular time in my life, and it took a lot of planning, thinking and negotiating to get it right. I couldn't afford to go off half-cocked and risk failure. You could certainly say that it scared me *every* day in the first few months!

Let me tell you: it's unbelievably daunting to open the doors of your business on the first day, and to realise that there is *not* an orderly queue of rich and willing customers outside. However, it was also, in a way, a great distraction from my then recent and painful personal history, and an opportunity for me to get back to where I felt I belonged.

Also, this path of destiny was *in my control*; no ill-informed middle managers were standing in the way of my success. There was just me and an office full of opportunity . . . and of course a lot of bravado!

The downside of my approach is that, as the business owner, you must understand that the buck stops with you and no one else. You also have to take into account the horrible truth that, just because you have given up paid employment to start your own business, it does not entitle you to reduce or stop your mortgage payments. Financially supporting your new business *and* your living costs will have to be built into your business plan's viability and sustainability.

This type of forward planning, taking into account all the factors that could go wrong or right, slower or faster than expected, applies to whatever course you plan to take. This could be remarriage, or cohabiting, or relocation, or a new job or indeed a new business start up. Whatever you choose, make sure you have sufficient ongoing income to cover your monthly liabilities, such as maintenance commitments.

As I'm sure you will have realised by now, this list of examples is endless. You are an individual and will lead a different life to every other person around you. Remember, it is *your* life and there is only one person who is going to live it: *you*.

The costs of being single

For some, the cause of the marriage break-up is another person; if this is not just a passing fling it may also mean that a new longer term relationship is already in place before the old relationship is finalised. This can mean a period of readjustment and transition from the old relationship to the new.

Any new relationship, whatever the circumstances, brings many new experiences, excitement and stresses. You may be in the process of managing the expectations of a previous spouse in knowing when you are available to look after the children, or to discuss who is getting what from the matrimonial home, whilst also trying to meet the needs and requirements of a new partner who may be at a different point in their own personal transition period.

One party may have left home to set up a new home with the other person to come and join. That change may have taken longer than expected. Or perhaps both jumped at the same time and are now trying to resolve the differences between four individuals, bringing significant stress to all parties and within the new union. This is where you need to think long and hard about the person with whom you are entering into a relationship, to ensure that this new love and companionship will not fall at the first obstacle.

You know any new relationship is going to be different from previous encounters and this should excite you. It's just a question of whether different is what you want long term, and they of you. This is an opportunity to test the commitment from your new love, so you can both be sure that there will be no early disappointments.

We are all different. There are people who prefer — or who have no choice but — to take a break from being a couple, and who spend some time on their own before seeking new companionship, if at all. By this, I do not mean that they don't enjoy a good social life or contact with friends and family; they simply take time out for themselves. This is always worth while. A new acronym I have recently heard is 'SAS'. It stands for Successful, Attractive and Single.

There is also a general longer term downward trend in the number of marriages taking place, with only 235,370 marriages in England and Wales in 2007, the lowest since 1895, in comparison to 480,285 UK marriages in 1972 (*source: Office of National Statistics*)

This makes sense when you think about how many people nowadays seem to marry later, live longer and live in single person households. The Office of National Statistics also notes on its website, www.ons.gov.uk, that there is a growing trend for people to live alone. This is borne out by a growth of 3.9 per cent from 1991-2001 in single person households. By 2006, no fewer than seven million households in the UK were single person households. To put this into context, around seventeen million were family households.

As with everything else, money may affect this decision. A survey in the summer of 2010, commissioned by the privately funded website, *www.uswitch.com*, suggests that the additional annual *premium* for being single each year is over £4,700, mainly due to additional housing costs. However, this report has drawn some criticism because there are so many different individual situations that it may not be as clear cut as the survey suggests. This will be affected by how you live, where you live and what you choose to do. However, it does highlight the fact that household bills now stop with you rather than are shared between yourself and a spouse.

Whichever route you take, budgeting your costs — either across a single income or across the finances of yourself and your new partner — is crucial to ensure that an early balancing of the household budget is achieved. Either or both of you may have commitments elsewhere, such as paying maintenance, and these will all need to be accounted for.

Also, don't forget to try and budget for a holiday. This might sound a low priority for now, but you will have been through a lot before you emerged blinking from the divorce 'tunnel' and it can be easy to forget that you also need a break from the immediate past. Good quality 'you' time is *not* a luxury, remember. Whatever way you decide to do it, build a holiday or at least a short break into the monetary equation.

You will have to take into account that, if you are travelling alone, your accommodation and other costs may rise because of the premium charged by many travel operators and hotels. You may have to compromise on your usual standards of location or accommodation level. Don't let that detail put you off taking a break at all, however.

I sentence you to another thirty years

Thinking ahead needs to take account of this year's personal budget and, in the longer term, some form of retirement strategy. This comes to us all; it's just a matter of how we choose to approach it.

It's all very well talking about the money; how long will you have to enjoy it?

The world is your oyster, the saying goes. Always remember that you can open an oyster and find a beautiful pearl — or just a lump of overpriced shellfish. Life can be more of a barnacle. You clutch on to existence with a vice-like grip, living off the detritus at the bottom of the rock pool.

You may have had a great relationship with your ex before you went your separate ways. The divorce might have been because you had just grown apart, rather than over some other issue.

In the subsequent mudslinging that was initiated after everyone else had stuck their oars in, there had grown a distinct dislike of your previous partner, pushing away any happy and valuable memories you might have had. These memories may have now vanished, and it is down to you to pick up the pieces. Or you might settle for an uneasy stalemate, but such an unresolved truce may not stand the test of time.

So, to be realistic, how long have you got to achieve your new plan of action?

The general health and wellbeing of the inhabitants of the UK has improved significantly over the last twenty-five years, especially for those in their middle and later years. It is only now that the health of our children could be turning out to be worse than our own, meaning that our children might live shorter lives than we will. This might be because of the more sedentary lives that they lead, with their computer games, 24-hour television and less sporting competition in schools. It may also be a reflection of the fast food diets and binge drinking our younger generation seem powerless to resist.

What are you spending?

I believe that you spend exactly two things at any given time in your adult life: time and money. The *money* can usually be recovered by means of a bit of attention, application and effort. The *time* can never be recovered; once spent, it is gone forever. However, do think long and hard about your *time expense* and check periodically whether you are wasting yours.

How long?

According to the Office of National Statistics, life expectancy has never been higher, with males living to over 77 and females to over 81.

What is interesting, if a little harder to understand, is that the longer you live, the longer you are likely to live *further*. UK statistics from 2006-2008 show that a man who lives to 65 is likely to live around another seventeen years on average, taking him up to the age of 82 or so; a woman's life expectancy starts to average out at 85 years old. Those living in England have the highest life expectancy and those living in Scotland, the shortest.

You can deduce what you want from these statistics, whether that be the differences between males and females and where you live in the UK — if indeed you plan to stay in the UK at all. These statistics will change over time in any case. The current prediction from the

Office of National Statistics is that life expectancy will continue to rise, at least for the time being.

What these statistics do start to show is that, if you were divorcing at age 45-50, you'd probably have a further 35 years to live. As you know, with a little application you can get an awful lot done in that time. In the example of someone aged 45, if you are in this position, think about how far you have got to date . . . and just about double it! This will give you a real indication of how long you have to achieve your aspirations.

This might change your expectations for the future, and start to put some perspective on what is possible in your individual circumstances. With the State Pension age increasing to sixty-six for males from 2016, and for all those reaching state pension age from 2020, for example, it is clear that we are all living longer and in many cases, working longer as well. This gives you the opportunity to maintain a better income for longer, possibly allowing your chosen lifestyle to be funded for a longer time as well. It is your call as to when you hope to retire; this will depend on your budget, your ability to save for retirement benefits or even the term of your outstanding mortgage, and maintenance agreement (which are usually time-bound) or children's university costs.

All these issues and more will need to be taken into account in your plans and adjustments made accordingly.

Pay attention

As I suggested earlier, this is not an exhaustive list of everything financial to which you should pay attention.

The points give you a flavour of what you might want to consider when looking at your money and finances in the new structure of your world. If in doubt, take advice; and most importantly of all, *take control*.

In my experience, many people find subjects like budgeting and pensions boring. Even I have to admit that, if you wanted to set the world alight with passion, you wouldn't start with either of those subjects. This does not reduce the importance of either subject; sticking your head in the sand and hoping that any financial problems will go away is not going to work.

In whatever way you want to think about and format your finances, make sure you do this early, even whilst the ink on the *Decree Absolute* is drying, to make sure that your recovery is not stilted by something as easily avoided as poor money management.

Your Notes

Consider and detail the parameters of your budget (income and outgoings) and your money planning here:

_____

_____

_____

_____

_____

_____

How often do you plan to review your money matters?

_____

_____

_____

_____

_____

_____

_____

_____

_____

Nagged, Tagged and Bagged...

Chapter Eight

Being comfortable on your own

Leopards don't change their spots. You may have been born to be single. You just needed to go through a marriage and subsequent separation to find this out for yourself. Alternatively, you may have been trapped in a marriage where your partner ruled the roost and you were, in effect, single anyway, with a piece of paper to say you were married.

Now that you are divorced or separated, you revert to type, being very comfortable in your own company. You may have to change your day to day thinking a bit, adjusting from the former norm of thinking for two, to thinking for one. This may take some time and you may make the odd mistake. But you should not feel in any way lonely, because you will not be on your own.

Do you doubt what I'm saying? Census data from 2001 showed that thirty per cent of households in England and Wales were single person households, divided almost equally between Pensioners and Others (source: Office of National Statistics) with the biggest rise across all households being the 'Others' section. With a total of just under 25 million households in 2001, that's about 7.5 million homes. Clearly, this is a growth sector.

Many people have little desire to roam these new 'single' pastures, but go on to find that their new single circumstances suit them anyway, at least at first. As time moves on they have no burning intention to leave behind the newfound freedom of being single.

Other people replace a lost partner with a pet to keep them company, and this can work well enough in many cases. As we all know, others cannot cope without human contact, both physical and emotional.

There are people who prefer to be alone and those who can't bear the thought of being single, possibly preferring others' company to their own. It seems to be like carrots, Marmite and the dark; you are either OK with it or you're not.

Which one are you?

I fall into the category of people not wanting to be alone — whereas I know many people who much prefer the freedom of a single life, even when they are married!

A divorce takes time to finalise itself. This gives you time to prepare to live on your own after the *Decree Absolute* is stamped by the court and delivered to your door.

In the case of the death of a partner, you are unlikely to have any notice or preparation time and your recovery may be stilted by the shock of bereavement. You might think that a comment on death is misplaced in this book; however, having spoken to a recently bereaved widow, the similarities between death and sudden separation are striking.

You will still need to look after yourself as you find your way round your new circumstances, and this in itself can be quite a task.

Supermarket sweep

I have always considered myself a modern man. As such, I am not unused to doing the weekly supermarket trawl round the aisles picking out the same products each week, with the occasional exciting BOGOFF (Buy One, Get One For Free) offer thrown in. I remember the first time I did this having just separated, and what a daunting affair it was; I must have looked like a startled bunny walking round the store, trying to learn the layout of this suddenly alien emporium.

First of all, the trolley I needed was different, being smaller and looking more like a handbasket on wheels than a grown-up shopping trolley. If you let it, you can become very conscious of the neon sign above your head flashing: '*single person shopping for one*' and which also allows you to spot at a glance all the other single folk in similar situations.

The forlorn look that speaks louder than words: '*How do you look after yourself healthily when shopping for one?*' steals across your face as you meander the aisles in the first few weeks, practising the art of staving off scurvy and any feral tendencies you may be suppressing. Also, the knowing glances from other *singletons* become apparent, almost like nods of camaraderie and defiance, which say: '*Yes, you look as if you survived as well.*'

This is starting to sound as surreal as *Supermarket Sweep*, a TV game show where you got to keep whatever you could stuff into your trolley within a set time. Funnily enough, some people seriously suggest that supermarkets are a great place to meet new people — almost a sweep of the store for possible suitors — because you can get an idea of what they are like from the goods in their basket or trolley. I remain *Undecided of Surrey* on this latter point.

However, making sure that you get into the discipline of stocking your food cupboards for one person with a balanced diet will enable you to make sure that you are correctly fuelled to face the new challenges that lie ahead of you. On your sweep of the supermarket, you might remember what you used to buy and what you did not buy because your ex-spouse did or did not like something. This knowledge was not just restricted to your shopping list, but also to all aspects of your shared lives, as you will see.

Knowledge of your ex-spouse

You might argue if you have known an individual for a few years, then you should know how they will react in various social, personal and business situations.

A good example of someone like this is your ex-spouse. You might know exactly how to irritate them and they you. You know which toys will be thrown out of which pram if any given event happens and you know that they would simply have laughed at some other situation or comment, had they been present. You will remember what they like to eat, where they like to eat it, what they like to wear, or drive. It may have been these points that drew you together in the first place or the things that finally drove you apart.

If you had been together for a long time, you may, inadvertently, call your new partner by your previous partner's name. This is a matter of habit rather than a sign of any subconscious longing for the past, and both you and your new partner should be prepared for this.

Future social etiquette

This is going to be a tricky subject at the best of times, especially if you had close family ties with your ex-spouse's family or have children from that marriage. You never know when you are going to bump into them, possibly stirring evocative memories that would have been better left alone.

Take as an example your favourite restaurant. The new love in your life decides to treat you to dinner at your favourite restaurant, whose only shortcoming is that it is occasionally frequented by your ex-spouse. You have not had the pleasure of bumping into them since the divorce but the waiters always look a bit awkward, knowing that two of their patrons may have an issue with each other. Nevertheless, the thought of the delicious gastronomy overcomes any apprehension and you turn up to find your ex-spouse in the corner table with their latest *squeeze*, looking every bit as loved-up as you had intended to be, prior to this moment.

An anxious dining experience is had by all, as each of the four parties involved is supremely conscious that the others are in the building. Exaggerated laughs and possible loud lustful kisses, with unnecessarily tactile behaviour, are observed across the restaurant by each party out of the corner of their eyes. The evening ends with stabbing stares as one party leaves, having hurriedly consumed their desserts.

A solicitor told me that a legal dispute was once launched on this very basis of the 'unnecessary' nature to which the new love had been 'flaunted' in front of the ex-spouse. I am sure that the meal left a bitter taste in all their mouths.

It is interesting that the man in the situation was completely unaware of the angst he caused to anyone else. He'd had a great time and had completely missed the need for social etiquette that should have been deployed in the situation which unravelled that evening.

He certainly knew about the situation by the time the dust had settled on the various solicitors' letters and the rather large invoice that resulted.

Thinking about social etiquette, the passage of time will be a factor — but do think forward to the day that your child gets married, graduates, or has a child of their own making you a grandparent (sorry to make you feel old!) . . . and then there may be your grandchild's christening or Bar Mitzvah or whatever rite of passage their parents choose to follow.

Are you going to be invited to any of these occasions if you can't be trusted to behave civilly? And what about the funeral of a loved one from the other side of what used to be your shared family? Do you attend the funeral or stay away and send flowers as a mark of respect? Even though you're divorced from your ex now does not mean they did not love you once, nor you them.

These tricky situations are bound to appear on your horizon at some point, and you will need to face them. You can't predict when any of them is sprung upon you.

Military crawl across the auction room floor

I like antiques. Many people do. I also like all things automotive, and find the merging of the two in an auction saleroom usually offers the opportunity for a bargain.

On one occasion, having received the monthly sale prospectus from the local auction house, I was surprised to see a rather tired looking, but nevertheless rare, 1974 chrome and mauve Kawasaki motorcycle for sale. The estimate seemed about right and I spent a few pleasurable days checking prices on the Internet to be sure this was as viable a project as I believed.

The sale was the following Tuesday and viewing was arranged for the Saturday morning. My wife also likes antiques and was unsurprised to see the rusting 'Kwacker' ringed as she looked through the other listings. A Saturday morning visit was agreed and I could barely contain my excitement as I hurried into the large but narrow barn-like sale room, jostling past the other punters and scampering down each aisle until I found the sad looking pile of rust at the back of the room, over to one side.

Nothing could distract me from prodding the mechanics, testing the brakes and checking the tyres and wheels. Esther, having spotted where I was, sauntered down to me. She was slightly fearful that if it bore any resemblance to a half decent mode of transport, then a large bid would be made and a purchase achieved, resulting in an assortment of pieces of motorcycle landing on our dining room table just in time for Christmas when the whole family descends on the house.

I had three or four minutes with the bike before Esther got near enough for me to explain the virtues of owning such a project. My mouth opened but nothing came out; I stood gaping past her to see, two aisles across, my ex-wife viewing some antiquity or other. Esther stared at me, fully expecting a gush of enthusiasm for the two-wheeled beauty, but not the mute goggling fool standing before her.

In slow motion I casually ducked out of view, closely inspecting the wheels of the motorcycle again, this time from ground level.

'Come on, what do you think of it?' Esther enquired, by now distinctly puzzled.

'Oh, hmmm! It's all right,' I muttered, my usually strong opinions totally quelled by the awkward situation. 'Take a look over there — the ex!' I mumbled quietly.

'Sorry, what?' was Esther's response, not entirely sure whether I was referring to some obscure piece of Japanese engineering.

'Over *there*. The ex-wife,' I hissed, indicating with my eyes in a pathetically childish manner.

Before Esther could turn around, I followed up with what felt like a perfectly reasonable question, far more pressing than buying some stupid motorcycle. 'How am I going to get out of here?'

Esther discreetly spotted the target of my tribulations before turning back to me and smiling charmingly. 'If you have to, go and sit in the car and then come back in when she has gone!' she suggested.

I smiled (I think it came across as more of a grimace) and smoothly employed an expertly-executed military crawl to make my undignified exit, only briefly pausing to look back at my two wives, one ex and one current, in the same room. My covert operation began to draw the attention of some of the sales staff, who must have thought I had a painting smuggled under my shirt!

Sitting in the car, luckily with blacked out windows, I started to feel rather embarrassed about the experience and I am sure one or two of you would agree. Couldn't I have been more grown up about this? It is after all a small world.

More importantly, what would you have done in those circumstances? Think about this for a moment. What would you like to think you would do and is the likely reality the same? After the event, I was disappointed by my actions and would not repeat them now, although I wish I had thought about the enevitablity of bumping into an ex before it happened.

Re-starting as you mean to go on

In re-starting a relationship with your ex-spouse or partner, which although uncomfortable may be required, you will have to think about both the longer term, as well as the now. There is always going to be a period of adjustment, but this will involve you knowing where you were, where you are now and where you want to be in the future.

If there are no children or other persons of the relationship, then the chances of bumping into an ex-spouse may only occur once in a while.

If there are children, contact may be once or twice a week, through child collections and alike. However difficult this may be at the start, your children are likely to benefit from continuity and harmony, both now and long into the future. Remember, time is a great healer. Your children may hope to go to university, get married and have their own children. Both parents will want to be there for them.

Re-starting your new separated relationship as you mean to go on may set the scene for years to come. Think about this and how you want this future contact to look. Your actions now may have a profound effect on the relationship that you have with your children, as an example, in years to come.

You might want to make some notes at the end of this chapter or in the exercise on the next page.

Exercise

Consider how you want your relationship with you ex-spouse to develop in the shorter term.

_____

_____

_____

How do you see your relationship in the longer term?

_____

_____

How are you going to communicate your thoughts to your ex- spouse, if needed?

_____

_____

Extra notes space has been made available at the end of this chapter.

Many people don't move far from their original location after a divorce. That being the case, there is some inevitability that you will bump into your ex-spouse in the most unexpected situations. You also have to think about any new partner you may be with, who may also not want to see your ex-spouse either.

If this is a second or third time round for both of you, you may also share a desire not to meet or bump into *any* ex-spouses, regardless of whose they are.

However, the first time is always the worst, if only because it brings back so many memories.

Ghosts in the machinery

The auction room incident is an amusing tale, although I have to say it did not seem remotely funny at the time (and I was outbid on the motorcycle) — but this raises the question of whether someone might inadvertently place a fictitious barrier on where you visit because of an imagined fear of bumping into a previous partner, unless contact with children is involved, as noted before.

At this point, you can call me a coward and I would happily agree I deserve it. Even I would probably convict myself of the same. But why did I react in such a bizarre way?

For me, my issue is that unexpected reminders of the past are not welcome and opening up a dialogue to that effect is likely to open old wounds that needn't have been opened — especially if they can be easily avoided. The life lessons have already been learned, but just like A-levels, I don't need to go back to the classroom to remember what I was taught.

How far does this avoidance strategy go? You have got to start living normally again, and if you are comfortable where you are, then go with what feels right for you. You can't live in anyone's shadow and you never should.

In chapter two (*Looking back*), we covered the issue of looking at the past in order to move forward. The rich experiences from which you learned then will stand you in good stead, possibly giving you a renewed sense of direction. But that is all they should do. Trying to *re-live* your memories, in my opinion, rarely works.

Some people completely avoid the potential for this contact situation by moving out of the area, although they may well still be collecting children from their previous neighbourhood. There will always be some retracing of steps in your life, but how this affects you boils down to the choices you want to make and where you want to be.

Whatever you do, be proud of who you are. We are all different, and each of us has different emotional and physical needs. Taking a break after a relationship to think about what you want from your future is vital. Finding an inner peace is a key to having confidence in moving forward.

As you know by now, being in a relationship is hard work. This hard work brings many benefits but it also brings many compromises, and as you grow older you may feel less prepared to accept compromise in your life. The steep rise in the number of single households in the UK in recent times is an indication of the desire of many people to stay single. Most people feel comfortable with this proposition and all its potential advantages and disadvantages.

Work-life balance

It's a common error to try to replace the void that may have been left in your personal time with work.

When you first separate from your spouse, it is very easy to find that gaps in your timetable that would have been filled by the demands of other people are now left free. Managing that time is important to ensure that you get some rest, in whatever form you prefer that to be.

The word *managing* is the important bit here. With the general pressures of life constantly upon us all, it is all too easy to find yourself working longer hours because there is no reason to go home to wherever you now live; because you're single now and there is no one to rush home to.

You may chuckle at this comment because the last thing you would want to do is work any longer than you have to, but many people throw themselves into work as a distraction from their personal situation.

Financial pressure may also make taking on an extra shift here or another project there more attractive, if not a necessity. It is not uncommon for work colleagues and managers who know about your new personal situation to 'help' you by offering extra work to take your mind off things. I could suggest that this is a lot like giving you a structure to hang onto while your personal life rearranges itself. It may also provide some welcome additional income. As you can probably guess, I find writing relaxing and cathartic. If you think you may be the same, then don't disregard its potential as a source of passive income and a good way to spend your spare time.

Although extra work may feel natural at first, make sure you keep it under control. At worst you could find that you set yourself a precedent that is neither sustainable nor good for you in the long run.

Always make sure that you get some 'down time' to cast off the pressure of your routine and to plan how your future will look. Many successful businesses have leaders who work 'on' the business, rather than 'in' it, always trying to focus on the bigger picture — a trait which can be frustrating for everyone else! You should think about doing the same with your life, because working every hour you can is only ever a short term solution.

Having fallen into the work trap myself, I can vouch for the fact that, although it offers some short term solutions and structure in a time of personal turmoil, it can be difficult to extract yourself later from the work *prison* that you create. That sympathetic manager who 'helped you out' may not be so sympathetic when you get your social life back and want to go back to a normal workload.

For those in any doubt, a regular dose of sitting in front of the television watching trash is not, in my opinion, good quality down time. You may disagree, but whatever you do, enjoy it.

Fits like a glove

Being single may simply be where you should always have been — you just needed to find that out for yourself. Alternatively, it may not be, however it suits you just fine anyway. Time will allow you to discover this and to also discover the shiny new you that you can be proud of.

Settling into your new regime may take a while and you will be relying on the one person that has never to let you down, namely *you*. Do what you want, when you want, how you want. This freedom should be exciting.

And if you are unexpectedly faced with the prospect of meeting your ex-spouse, then react professionally and move on. They probably will too.

You will be the better person for it.

Your Notes

Were you born to be single? If not, what do you want from a relationship and why?

_____

_____

_____

_____

_____

How will you react on meeting ghosts from your past?

_____

_____

_____

_____

What relationship, if any, do you want with your ex-spouse into the future and why?

_____

_____

_____

_____

Nagged, Tagged and Bagged...

Chapter Nine

Church, House and Mr Lightyear

Having written it, this book feels to me as if it has reached to infinity and beyond. Just when you thought that you had your plans and objectives mapped out and your confidence has been restored, you can probably guess, it turns out that I have *not* quite covered everything.

Considering your divorce recovery stages made so far, you will know that you may not have two pennies to rub together, that the change process is hard work and that you are maintaining a watchful eye on your health as you sit on the sofa sipping a large glass of red wine and munching calorific snacks. Further adventures lie ahead but you are recovering — honest, you are!

In the mêlée of working on the issues already dealt with in your day to day life, yet more subjects may come on to the agenda as you progress. Some may not bother you in any positive or negative way because of your individual circumstances.

Each of the divorce recovery stages we have looked at so far are *practical*. However, you may find the next few points more emotive. You may find that they affect the most important areas in your life and have the greatest effect.

Religion

I am not a religious man, although I was up to my mid to late twenties. I didn't feel that I could write a book about divorce recovery without touching on this subject. Rather than talk about the various sectors of religion, I would like to talk about the impact a divorce can have on your continued faith and also on the way that others in a congregation to which you belong may respond to your situation.

You may feel that this is nothing to do with them, only with the God you worship; in my opinion you would be correct. However, others may see things differently — and if you look to those people within your religious group for support and comfort, you may be sorely disappointed or find this a terrific help. I hope it is the latter.

Perhaps you're going to discuss your position with an elder, vicar, or some other respected individual. Whoever you decide to confide in, first be sure that you completely trust them. If your faith is an integral part of your life and needs for the future, ensure that you know what that person's view of your marital position is likely to be.

In your overall plans to renew yourself after your divorce, you may plan to relocate various things, such as work or social scene or home. You may want or need to add your place of worship to that ever-growing list of changes. I am not referring to your faith as such, just the location where you choose to spend time with the one you believe in.

This may not be part of your plan, although if your ex-spouse went to the same church, there may be little choice. This could work to your advantage in meeting new like-minded people sharing the same values as you. However, some people believe firmly in the sanctity of marriage whatever the circumstances, and will not feel able to accept your new situation. This may be your biggest test of faith, so be ready to face up to it.

Reading this book right now, this section may be an irrelevance to you and I accept that. However, there are others for whom it may be the most important factor in their overall recovery.

Old friends and neighbours

The poison of spite can often flow freely during the divorce process and many vile words can be spoken of either spouse to anyone who listens. It is not uncommon to bump into old friends and neighbours who you had had a good relationship with, only to find that their view of you has been tainted significantly by the views of others in the heat of battle. Your friendly approach to greet an old acquaintance is met with an icy 'hello' and 'hope you are well', before moving away as speedily as they decently can.

In approaching this situation, be prepared to rise above it. You may have had nothing to do with the opinion that has been formed of you, and it is mainly their loss not yours, however hurtful it may first appear. They are in the wrong, not you.

Other friends will be delighted to see you. They will have been able to think for themselves about your real situation, counting the days since they last saw you. Obviously, there are always those who cannot or, possibly stubbornly, refuse to be prepared to believe anything other than what they are told by other people. These are acquaintances you should be pleased to lose.

Is divorce contagious?

Recent long term research from America does suggest that divorce can be *contagious*. For reference, the research and subsequent study paper is entitled: *"Breaking up is hard to do, unless everyone else is doing it Too: Social Network Effects on divorce in a longitudinal sample followed for 32 years"* by Professor James H. Fowler of UC San Diego.

This can raise the question of whether divorces can manifest themselves in *Clusters? Cluster divorces* can be defined where within a social network group, one couple gets divorced and this makes others in their group question their relationships with the corresponding fallout of further divorces, may make some individuals nervous about maintaining contact with someone who has recently completed the divorce process.

You may have experienced this situation, however, some are sceptical of the reality of this possibility.

Adjustment

Your new beginning is going well. You have survived the loss of a partner and maybe a family; you may find it hard to believe, but this is when you need to be open to new opportunities. Your leisure time is also going to change as you explore new pastimes that you may have not considered for years. As the back of the book suggests, 'let's explore'.

This may be on your own or with a new companion and will take you to places and make you do new things that you had never anticipated.

After my second divorce, I met and eventually set up home with my third wife, Esther. This was an enjoyable experience, even though money was extremely tight and the creativity in making the budget balance kept both of us awake at night — and not for the reasons we might have hoped!

It is interesting, adjusting your own style to accommodate a new person into your life. I can understand why so many people find the pressure of this change too much and decide that they are not going to be as flexible as is required to achieve the compromise required to be a couple again. Maybe because they can't see the benefit of the co-existence being offered, or perhaps they have been so scarred by relationships in the past that they dare not risk the anguish of a potential separation in the future. Or it might be just bloody-mindedness.

Each of you will know your own innermost feelings and it would pay you to be honest with yourself about these.

Stability

The house Esther and I rented was as good we could afford in our relatively meagre financial circumstances, providing us with stability to reset and reassess our futures, either together or in other directions. In my opinion, we owe a lot to this stability. We rented the house for around eighteen months in the end, before moving to another rented house (which turned out to be a wrong move) and then buying our own bricks and mortar.

Moving home, whether buying or renting, takes a lot of time, effort and usually money. Of these, it is the energy and time cost that I am most concerned about, especially in the divorce recovery stage.

At the risk of repeating myself, you are always spending two things: one is time and one is money. This is important because lost money can be recovered over time with a bit of fiscal focus, but time can never be regained. There are many situations and people in life who will gladly *steal* your time in return for no benefit to you. I call them *time stealers*, and you should remember this concept when you next meet someone and wonder where on earth you are going or, possibly more concerning, what on earth you are doing with them.

Imagine your time is a bank account. Let's say someone had found out your PIN and could take out a few hundred pounds, without asking your permission. Would you let them get away with it? I don't think so. So from your *time bank*, why let them have your access codes to use up your valuable time? Your time is every bit as valuable as your money.

Stability of accommodation and employment affords the opportunity of personal time to think about how you want your future to look before making any changes. With Esther's support and help, both physical and financial, we decided after a year of contemplation to set up our own company, as noted before. Much spare time was spent plotting, planning and enquiring about all things business. But time to achieve all this was possible only because we were no longer moving from place to place. However, the budget was still incredibly tight.

If you think about your own future stability, this could be in various situations and circumstances. What would this look and feel like for you?

Exercise

What is stability to you?

_____

_____

_____

Where would this be?

_____

_____

_____

Why is stability important to you?

_____

_____

_____

Extra notes space has been made available at the end of this chapter.

Holiday in my head

Esther and I took up a few new hobbies that we would not normally have considered, either because of the lack of time in previous relationships, or because these hobbies had not been an option in the past.

We both studied Art to A-level standard, neither of us having visited the subject since leaving education. We started an adult education course locally, one night a week, making small silver jewellery pieces. This course had many advantages, although at the time turning out at 7.00pm on a Monday night in the pouring rain after a full day's work was not something we looked forward to.

However, it was a very therapeutic process. It carved out some personal time in the weekly calendar to create something, and to let our brains deal with something completely alien to our normal business world. The class was cheap, we got to meet new people and share new ideas, try out new artistic techniques in 'silversmithery' and usually have a beer with classmates on the way home.

This time became like a 'holiday in my head' in the normally busy week, where I could let my mind wander, without fear of interference from the outside world. Even such brief relaxation, at a stressful time in life, cannot be valued too highly.

I built a silver design piece, based on the gyration of the planets and satellites. Borrowing a lyric from the late Kirsty McColl, I called it 'Wishing on Space Hardware'. It had a cheeky illustrated grin from Mr Buzz Lightyear from the movie Toy Story in the corner, against a backdrop of stars. As the fictional character suggests, '*to infinity and beyond*' can be a perfectly reasonable aspiration, although I am sure he was aiming higher than an evening silversmith class during a damp and cold winter.

Esther and I also took up scuba diving. Admittedly this came later in our marriage once the budget allowed, but was another example of something completely different that neither of us had experienced before. It brought back no memories from our previous relationships and was purely about us.

Does this last point matter? It certainly added a fresh new dimension for both Esther and I to share. We worked together towards passing the various tests and are now able to go deeper and deeper underwater and see more of the world from a completely different perspective; one I very much enjoy. I must admit that I do get nervous when the sharks are bigger than me, especially when they circle you at 100 feet below the waves. I understand that it's only when they start to *bump* you that you have to worry.

Back to school?

Your scope is not limited to leisure activities. I know *academia* sounds like an illness; however, a return to education might be a good idea. You can undertake a course or study to suit the *new* you.

This idea did not appeal to me at all because I was never academic at school. I left school with a few O-levels and a couple of A-levels, mainly in art-based subjects. I had a great time at school, learnt little, although the oil paintings were good and I still have some to prove it, and then went out to work.

Post divorce, having researched, committed to and then taken up a course, I finished my distance learning degree in Financial Services two years later. I didn't even know you could get a score in a degree until the last year; I understand a 2:1 is not a bad outcome. It certainly gave me a great sense of achievement and revealed to me that I liked writing. That's why you are currently reading the third book in the *Churchouse Chronicles*.

Also, by the time I had reached my mid-thirties, I knew what I wanted to do, what I was good at and, most importantly, what I enjoyed. You can do the same, in whatever way suits you best.

Do a GCSE or an A-level or a degree or diploma. Learn a new language, play an instrument or join a football team. Many people find that rediscovering of an old hobby or a musical instrument can be very inspiring.

These are only a few examples of the different activities, hobbies and pastimes that can be considered in your new life. You may not like the sound of any of these, and that would be only natural. However, do think about something you have always wanted to do, or something you used to enjoy when you were younger. Does it rekindle a fire that was extinguished by the previous pressures of life?

You will know what is right for you. Be under no illusion that your time will fill up very quickly, so make the most of any thinking time you have available. You might choose to take up motorcycling, writing, music, painting, fitness; you name it. Whatever the chosen pastime, make sure that you give yourself this release, your own *holiday in your head* to relax, let your mind wander and discover more about yourself.

How far can you go?

Relocation, relocation

The television programme of the same name supports the benefits of a planned relocation and sensibly tries to highlight the pitfalls of taking any geographical swap on board. As illustrated in the surveys of *Holmes & Rahre*, as mentioned in chapter four, *Stress*, a house move and divorce come highest in the rankings of the most stressful points in anyone's life, along with bereavement and an employment change. Some people see a divorce as bereavement anyway; although nobody actually died, something probably shrivelled within someone's heart, with some memories being laid to rest.

At any time when dreams of the past are dashed, it is good to refocus on new aspirations — possibly in a new location, possibly a new *life junction*?

You may not want to think about this so soon after divorcing. But, why do you live where you do? Do those reasons still hold true?

For some people, the location of the old home was always a practical compromise. It might have been an equidistant point from two places of employment, with each party travelling about the same distance to work every day. Take a look at the hordes who commute into London by train and you can quickly work out that anywhere within an hour's journey of central London (or any other major city for that matter) commute from areas that could be your potential new home town.

Was the final compromise of your old home *your choice* all that time ago? Would you now like to correct that issue — subject to maintaining suitable access to children if this is a factor in your circumstances?

This *life junction* gives you the opportunity to review that choice of location, whether to dismiss it or to find that it's still the right one. This is your fresh start and a change of scenery may be just what the doctor ordered.

Should you happen to work for a large company, consider applying for a relocation package. This would move your career away from its old location, and your employer might even help towards the removal cost? It might also enable your employer to see you in a new light, as you demonstrate that you are flexible about working elsewhere; that sort of move could move you up the ranks and corresponding salary scale. Of course, this may be subject to many other issues, such as future contact with children.

Talking of relocation costs, this opportunity may realistically be restricted by budget. On the other hand, you may need to move to an area that offers greater value for money because of maintenance costs or loss of capital in the final *Financial Settlement*.

In the climate of recession, mortgage lending criteria have tightened and the ability to borrow may be restricted. Expect further irony when the affordability calculations are applied to your future mortgage application. Some providers will deduct liabilities from your income, such as maintenance payments, before calculating the amount you can borrow, possibly restricting the type of property available to you. Also, if you are *receiving* maintenance, don't assume that it will be automatically included within your budget allowance when the lender is calculating affordability.

Because of these factors, you may want to check the mortgage situation promptly in order to understand your individual position.

Having considered all the pros and cons that matter to you, if you do decide to relocate to a new area, then you have the options of buying or renting. Most people will be delighted to share their opinions on this subject. However, it is important to remember that this is your individual road to divorce recovery and no one else's.

If you don't know the proposed new area well, you might consider renting for six months or so, to understand the good and the bad points and give you time to work out where is best for you. The factors to consider may include the proximity to work or facilities, schools and colleges, and distance from other family members.

Your choice might be profit motivated, looking at trying to achieve a small property development to increase your capital levels. You know what you want to achieve, so don't rush into a decision that you might regret. Property mistakes are usually costly, especially if you decide to move again quickly.

Renting has its down sides as well. It means moving your belongings in and then out again, possibly in quick succession. This can make some people feel as if they're living out of a box. However, the upside is that it gives you the flexibility to have a hunt around and discover new areas which you may have not known about before moving.

Relocation is not possible for everyone, however for many people it provides a welcome chance to put distance between themselves and their past. All experience provides knowledge that can be used to improve your own situation in the future. Relocation also provides some with the confidence to walk down the local High Street without the fear of bumping into the ex-spouse or a now ex-relative. This factor might be all the more relevant if you are now in a new growing relationship with your new partner, and don't want past baggage getting in the way of this exciting chapter in your life.

All of which leads us to consider how you are going to create time for a new social network, if that is what you want.

Time bandits

Invasion of your privacy is galling at the best of times, no matter how it happens. If it comes from members of your own family it really can get your hackles up, however well intended it may be.

You know perfectly well that your parents will want to enjoy their natural affection for their grandchildren and have their opportunity to influence your children's growing up process, passing on further wisdom from where they left off with you. Beware of the warning signs if this becomes overwhelming.

Family and close friends will know that you are in recovery mode after a death or divorce, coping with facing this where you are now on your own. You may naturally be grateful for some help — but do proceed with caution.

The offer of help and support, which may be very welcome at an emotionally difficult time, may be all the more powerful if you have children, especially young ones. Helpers will want to 'take them off your hands' or 'have them over to stay, while you sort yourself out'.

It is important to remember that rebuilding your life must include your children who are going to take this journey with you. They are your children after all. It can be too easy to find your well-meaning parents or other relatives interfering with your valuable personal time and, for example, controlling the outcome of your weekend or evenings; or worse, holidays!

This could involve their descending on your household at limited notice to do something *nice* with your kids and you; perhaps taking them on holiday or asking you to drop them off at their house. This may suit you at the time, but it will take the initiative away from you. It is your role to ensure that any such arrangements fit with your own expectation of how the future will look for both you and your children, otherwise those helpful family members may become *time bandits*.

'Time theft' needs to be controlled at an early stage of the divorce recovery process. It's easy for anyone to forget the boundaries of a relationship, and for those boundaries to be breached and re-set at a point that may not suit you after a while.

You may not have realised that your personal boundaries have moved, because you are operating as a single unit. Where were your boundaries before you became a divorcee? Have they been prescribed over time by your ex-spouse? If this was the case then you may want a quick refresher in your own mind as to your ethics and the persuasions that suit you and your new style.

This situation can be exacerbated if you only get to see your children every other weekend.

You might be picking them up after work on a Friday night and dropping them back on Sunday afternoon, leaving you about thirty-six hours in between to reconnect with your loved ones. Interruptions to this precious time need to be handled carefully, especially in the early recovery stages, as your children will also be trying to adapt to this new limited contact regime. None of it may come naturally at first.

Their time with you is as precious to them as it is to you and they may have been waiting two weeks to tell you what has been happening in their lives. Think about this carefully and make sure that you give each other time to catch up properly.

One significant blow that could hamper your recovery is if you lose contact with your children for any reason. A BBC documentary, *Who Needs Fathers? The Right to Be a Dad* (2010), detailed statistics that showed that fathers who lose contact with their children (nearly 40 per cent), usually do so within two years of separation.

You should take into account your changing lifestyle and circumstances, and that of your ex-spouse who is also likely to move on. Consider having some family photos taken so that, if you do part company, you have something to remember them by until, hopefully, you meet again when they reach adulthood. Time bandits arrive before you know it and you need to be prepared. You can always just say: '*No!*' firmly at the outset; however, if their help might be useful in the future then you may not want to bite the hand that is trying to help you. Is this being selfish? It's your journey, and in the recovery stage, selfish is good.

Alternatively, if you are going to give *time bandits* some space so that they can be of help, then you might want to lay out a few parameters, such as the time available and when they are leaving. One easy way round this is to visit *them* first, giving you the control as to when you leave. You have to be a bit harsh, and if they really care for you then they would not want to outstay their welcome. They will understand that you need your space to think, see other people, see your children on your own, and find out for yourself where you want to go.

Alternatively, you might just need time to yourself to cry or get angry, both of which are parts of the bereavement process and your recovery. You may remember this from chapter three about *emotional signposting*. These are perfectly natural phases and it is unlikely that you will be able to move on successfully without saying goodbye to the past and accepting its outcome.

This might sound a bit trite after the battle that you have just had to get divorced — but there are usually *some* good memories, emotions and times that you will miss. These need to be reflected on and accepted before packing them away and moving on. This is all part of the process of your healing and recovery.

Time bandits are everywhere and are ready to take a slice out of your life if you don't lay out your boundaries early. Be ready to ensure that you get the best out of them for your situation. The people who love you will understand; those that don't weren't worth knowing in the first place.

Happily ever after

Unlike a child's fairy tale, life can have a habit of not ending happily ever after. You know this by now and you are, I hope, ready for it. This chapter has focused on some of the more obscure and possibly emotive aspects of divorce recovery that may not have been immediately on your radar.

This is only a flavour of what you need to consider. You will see some of these points occurring in your recovery in one form or another, and you will have to keep managing your expectations as you go along.

The key here is to prepare for the challenges that face you, and to be willing to change your assumptions about the future ahead, in whatever you are involved in. Change the word 'group' to 'club' or 'team' and the location of Central London to Birmingham, Torquay or Carlisle. Whichever details in this book you change to fit your own experience, the meaning and the messages remain. As long as you can take these 'wrinkles' into account your recovery will remain on track.

Whatever you do, *give yourself time*. This is your divorce recovery and no one else's. It is a special time, although it may not feel like it right now.

Your Notes

What have you never done before that you want to do now? What's your motivation?

How will you control your time for the things that you want to do?

How have you prepared for these challenges?

Chapter Ten

Opportunity knocks

Do you remember the TV game show *Opportunity Knocks*? It was originally presented by Mr Hughie Green from the studios of Thames Television and if you remember all that then you are showing your age.

Now in my mid-forties, I can just remember him presenting this TV talent show. I was only 10 when it went off air in 1978. Clearly the issue of finding new talent could not be suppressed, and the show was re-introduced by the BBC twice, from 1987-1989 (Bob Monkhouse) and in 1990 (Les Dawson). They have now all been replaced with fast-moving replicas as evening entertainment.

It was less the show's talent-finding format than its catchy name that made me think of the phrase, *Opportunity Knocks*.

Opportunity does knock for us all, every day of our lives and in everything we do. How we play the game determines how we win. Sadly, there are no big cash prizes, no family car or speedboat to be won in our day to day lives. *'And I mean that most sincerely!'*

The UK's love of talent shows seems not to have waned. In today's terms, a similar prime time talent show would be *X Factor*. People from far and wide come to display their talent, dressing the part, getting it wrong a few times and having a laugh about it, then getting through to the next round, mainly judged by those around them.

Hang on a minute! That sounds rather like all the things we do as individuals in our day-to-day lives, interacting with everyone around us — whether that be our marriage, divorce, employment, social circle or other personal communication. We just need to be *discovered*.

For your own performance, where the stage is yours alone, I am sure you will make sure that you identify your particular target; audition for the role of friend, colleague, partner or spouse; occasionally make a fool of yourself; win the round with the best parts of your personality and charisma; and go on to the next round, polishing your act the further up the rankings you go.

Life as a talent show

This raises the question: is life one big talent show? Well, yes!

You choose your costume (could be a suit, uniform or overalls), you polish your *act* to ensure that it is delivered in the way you want it to come across, and hope that the audience you have chosen approves. When you get a low score, you come back next time until the panel you are asking to judge you awards you full marks.

The reality is most of us are not doing it for the cameras or to seek fame and fortune, but to find love, peace, happiness and some success.

Our whole business and work lives are now performance-driven. Success is judged less on the effort you put in than on the final outcomes. The past is important in that it helps to teach us for the future — but, in business as in most life situations, it is here-and-now where everyone wants to see sustained progress.

We spent a few pages looking at change and its effects in chapter five. Change is a great thing if you control its direction and outcome. And do remember that change doesn't have to be a big jump; a subtle adjustment can do the trick.

You will have thought about what you want to achieve in this new segment of your life. You now know that you are usually only spending two things in life, which are money and time. Both are as valuable as each other, so use them wisely. The drama you have just been through may be one of a series of situations that you will have to first cope with, and then conquer to grow from thereafter.

As you now know, I have been through the divorce process twice. When I got married, I had truly hoped that there would be no divorce to follow. As you also know, two divorces later, a new era in my life started. Voids were filled, acceptance understood, expectations amended and dreams refocused. It all took time and I believe that the outcome has been worthwhile.

Now it's your turn to brush yourself down, put a sticking-plaster on, heal the emotional cuts and bruises (and hopefully not physical injuries) that you may have sustained, and move your life forward into the next exciting phase.

The next part of your life, too, is a phase. There will be many more to follow in the course of your journey and recovery. Like the chapters of this book, each phase is different and there may be seven, eight, ten or different types of change 'chapters' on your own or with others in your life. Writer and social ecologist, Peter F Drucker, once said of change: *'One cannot manage change. One can only be ahead of it.'*

In leading your own life, you need to know which page you are on, to make sure that you can manage its outcome and move forward to the next pages and chapters.

Just remember to make a few notes as you go because your individual recovery will be different to mine and everyone else's and you cannot flick over chapters in your life without being true to yourself.

Mood control

Have you ever thought about choosing your mood?

Some mornings you get up thinking the world is a great place and that life is going to work for you today. On other days, you fall out of the wrong side of the bed, in darkness even in the height of summer, as if Lucifer himself had become your best buddy overnight.

The effects of rejection or obsession can make you struggle to find your sense of humour; this is another phase that you will overcome in time. With some considered application, you can train and control your moods, selecting from a range of positive options. You might think this is a bit facile — and admittedly, for some it is easy and for others impossible.

Think about your day so far. How did you feel this morning when you awoke? Has your day moulded itself around this first impression, or has your mood changed and did you control that change? If you did, how did you do it? Could you do it again, every day, even on bad days?

I hope that your answer is *yes please!* You've just got to try it and see.

Thinking about the day you have had today, whilst reading this book, has it worked out the way you wanted. And if not, what would you change?

The exercise overleaf may help you with your progression

Exercise

What was your mood when you awoke this morning?

Did this mood change and why?

What would you do differently if you had today again?

Will the answers to these questions help you tomorrow morning?

Extra notes space has been made available at the end of this chapter.

The work of the painter Picasso went through a number of phases, including the famous 'cubist' and 'blue' periods, each named for the colours or themes he used as he moved through the experiences and moods of his life, embodying these in the form of fine art. It has been suggested that the factors at play in his life whilst painting could be as extreme as illness or love, different partners or even locations. But each phase reflects the artist's changed circumstances or moods as they were experienced.

When you are a recovering divorcee, the virtues that once attracted the partner that you spent the previous phase of your life with may have been dulled by time, angst and bickering. The solicitors' bills will have done nothing to help. This is all behind you now, although the memories of the encounter will be fresh and may linger some time.

The next exciting phase of your life has begun and its path is yours to map. We have looked in some depth at your recovery and at the points you will need to consider in making this happen. This will take time and there is no hurry; if there *is* a sense of urgency about it, then that is your decision.

It went wrong for you once before, but that is just a fading memory for you. It's in the past. That does not mean that you have not learnt a few lessons from the encounter. You will be emotionally wiser and (probably) financially poorer for the experience. You are going to get it right in the future, and you now know what this is going to look like.

You will recover, in time. You will find peace again, although you may have to figure out what *peace* means for you; when you find it, I hope you will smile. All this will take effort from you, and desire to make your act the very best on the stage of life that you appear on.

Reflection

Our time together during this book has been one of reflection, planning and looking forward to a brighter future. You might also call it a reality check on your new life. It should have allowed you to focus on the need to set yourself some positive goals that you can seek to achieve, to help you reach a new level of personal satisfaction and inner confidence. What targets have you chosen?

I have detailed how any target you set can be reached, by putting in place a step-by-step decision making process and actions, to allow you to chart your progress towards them. *'Do something that scares you every day'* as both I and Esther in her Foreword have suggested before, it is always a good challenge.

As examples of stepping outside my own comfort zone, I completed the Great South Run in 2008, admittedly quite slowly; appearing for book signings in local bookstores was also up there in the scary stakes for me. If you are living within a comfort zone, you may be on a collision course with mediocrity. This is fine if it's what you want, but you know you can achieve more — and you now have the tools to do it. How are you going to step outside your comfort zone?

I was born with Spina Bifida, which is why I support the charity ASBAH on the back cover of all of my books. In my mind, this condition made me an underdog from the start. My impression of life was that I had to work harder than those around me just to match them. I now realise that this was not actually the case; however, the upside of my misguided thoughts is that my life has had far greater fulfilment than if I had taken a more *laissez-faire* attitude to each hurdle life threw at me.

Admittedly, this view of life has the downside of never being truly satisfied with even the best of outcomes because there is always a nagging doubt that you could have done better. However, it does let me think outside the box most of the time, whilst also giving me energy to fulfil my objectives.

Think about your own situation, what you have achieved and what do you plan to do?

This new outlook is applicable to everything you do and whatever objective you want to set yourself. So, at this point of reflection, are the targets you have set yourself really likely to happen?

You know who you are and, even with the possible setback or release of a divorce, who you want to be in the future. You never lost the virtues of who you are at your core, and even if your ex-partner regrets ever letting you go, they are never going to admit this now. The life lessons you have survived will stand you in good stead.

One happy reflection for me was the experience of writing this book. The enthusiasm with which my contacts engaged in my simple survey was inspiring, because of the energy that they showed in the way that they had moved on. I would like to thank them for their input (and they know who they are). Their views really did add a different perspective on the outcomes actually achieved in the book.

It's true that from the survey results, I was anticipating sorrowful tales of how difficult the transition can be. What I was not expecting was the sheer drive and enlightenment that all of them felt. And I do mean *all* of them: the release and ability to find themselves again has given me confidence that the purpose of writing this text to share with you has been truly worthwhile.

New wisdom

We have considered why the environments that we grew up in will fashion our views of the future. Of course your old partner, and the baggage that you carry from your union with them, will have an effect on your thinking, but I hope that we have been able to separate out this influence to allow you to see which knowledge is useful and what can be 'stored' at this stage.

Any knowledge has value, it's just a question of when you use and apply it. This wisdom has the power to give you understanding and inner peace. Make sure you use it to your advantage as you settle into the new life that you create for yourself. You could argue that the 'advantage' of your divorce was that you learnt a lot.

One way of letting yourself down is by *not* using this experience to improve your prospects and success. If you remember my thoughts about *life junctions* in the introduction of this book, you will know where you have been, where you are now and the directions you can go in next. Using your wisdom to guide you will mean that you make the right choices.

You also need to consider that your divorce recovery will never stop, only develop and evolve further, with many more *life junctions* along the way. As an example, if you think about the years that will tick by, the first year might be finding your feet and making any financial budget work for you. The next year might find you expanding your horizons on all fronts, having spent a year assessing where you'd landed after your divorce. The third year might see you making emotional and physical moves with new people, new pastimes or work commitments. This might not be the case if you had left your marriage or partnership for another person, although this will still mean that you will not stop your journey of development.

It's almost like a business plan, with the objective of propelling you down a production line and adding new and improved features to your overall product.

Having achieved a greater degree of recovery (as I have discovered), you may well be in a position to share your experiences with others to help them with their own situation. I know many parents who have coached children and relatives (whether parents have been divorced or not) through the maze of recovery. I think that for some it takes them back to when their children were children, and re-teaching them the virtues of life and the boundaries that are there to be explored.

This new found wisdom can be helpful to others, even if it is just to provide some solace in the early times in knowing that they are not alone.

Don't get this mixed up with the individuals for whom the most exciting thing that has ever happened to them is that they got divorced, thus giving them the *right* to relive it with you or anyone else that will listen. I sometimes refer to them as *divorce bores,* as I noted in my second book, *Journey of Divorce. Addicted to Wedding Cake.* True experience and well founded delivery of such wisdom is always welcome. However, wallowing in an event that has taught *them* nothing will only drain *you* of energy.

Instruction manual

Your die was cast all those years ago; it's just that you have spent all this time putting together the instruction manual to understand how to use 'you' properly.

Going back to your childhood, you may remember getting a toy or kit model and trying to assemble the object without the instruction manual, usually left in the box or flung across the room, only returning to it when the manufacture of your dream toy has no resemblance whatsoever to the box cover or your dream. That *bingo!* moment happens when you turn to page four and realise that part B-iii does not fit in slot C-iv and that if you move it to slot B-ii, all will be well (as long as you haven't already glued it in place!).

Having been through the divorce experience myself, I can say with some authority that recovery is a great adventure. You will discover many good things about your own personality that have never have come into focus before. Sure, I have made more than my fair share of mistakes along the way and this is only part of the overall process. Other personality traits may have been in sharp focus for years but you'd never understood their effects both on your life and on those around you. You may want to enhance or control these traits — that's your choice.

The passing months and years change your perception, as you mellow into who you really are. And now you know how, this should have a positive effect on your outlook on the future.

Turning now to you and your own divorce recovery, I wish you every success with your new and exciting journey as you explore your talents, developments, possible shortfalls and aspirations. Although you may be nervous or bewildered as you face the prospect, I hope that you are genuinely excited by the opportunity of building a life that really suits you, rather than only suiting those around you.

All you have to do is get your instruction manual out and read it!

So, finally, are you ready to step into the spotlight for the *talent show* of your recovery?

Have you chosen the venue and audience? Of course you know that the act you are about to perform will have them leaping out of their seats. You positively exude confidence and self belief. The costume you have selected looks fantastic and just right for the occasion. Do you know when you have to be there and have you left enough time for one last run-through of your show?

Just remind me of your killer punch line that is going to knock your audience dead. . ? *Great!*

Your audience is ready and, like you, excited with anticipation and now — it's your turn.

Opportunity knocks! Good luck.

Your Notes

Are you ready for your recovery? Are you clear on what you want to acheive? When are you going to achieve them? Finalise your recovery plans here.

Your opportunity knocks! Good luck.

Resources:

Office of National Statistics. Website for the UK of national statistics.

Full details and information at the website, *www.statistics.gov.uk*

Also, www.ons.gov.uk

Holmes TH, Rahe RH (1967. "The Social Readjustment Rating Scale"

Social Readjustment Rating Scale (SRRS) USA. A study of the prediction of near-future health change from subjects' preceding life changes

Sexually Transmitted Diseases (STDs) Health Protection Agency Research. Published in the Journal, AIDS, July 2010

HIV Transmission and high rates of HIV diagnosis among adults aged 50 years and over. AIDS 2010, *Smith RD, Delpech V, Brown AE, Rice BD*

Health Protection Agency: Centre for Infections Research

Article '*HIV infection more than doubles in over 50s' July 2010*'

Full details and information at the website, *www.hpa.org.uk*

Cluster Divorces research and subsequent study paper
is entitled: *"Breaking Up is Hard to Do, Unless Everyone Else is Doing it Too: Social Network Effects on Divorce in a Longitudinal Sample Followed for 32 Years"*

Professor James H. Fowler of UC San Diego (McDermott/ Fowler/Christakis).

*(Also Falling in love costs friends/***Newspaper Articles/ September 2010)**

Study by Professor Robin Dunbar professor of Evolutionary Anthropology at Oxford University. Study to be released in late 2010.

Between– and Within–sex Variations in Hormonal Responses to Psychological Stress in a Large Sample of College Students

The Journal, *Stress, Stress 2010, Chicago University and North Western University. Study of Cortisol and its effects.*

Dario Maestripieri, Professor in Comparative Human Development at the University of Chicago.

Who Needs Fathers? The Right to be a Dad (2010) BBC documentary

Study by **Professor Huston (Professor of Human Ecology at the University of Texas)** in the US Journal, *Personal Relationships*

Moving on up (2009), Mental Health Foundation

The Foundation has published a report in 2009, called 'Moving on up', which raises awareness obout the positive benefits that exercise can have on mental health.

www.mentalhealth.org.uk

Nagged, Tagged and Bagged...

Useful websites

Mind

www.mind.org.uk

Mind helps people to take control over their mental health. This is to make it possible for people who experience mental distress to live full lives, and play their full part in society. It provides information, advice and training programmes.

Relate

www.relate.org.uk

Relate offers advice, relationship counselling, sex therapy, workshops, mediation, consultations and support face-to-face, by phone and through their website.

Mental Health Foundation

www.mentalhealth.org.uk

Founded in 1949, the Foundation is a leading UK charity that provides information, carries out research, campaigns and works to improve services for anyone affected by mental health problems, whatever their age and wherever they live.

Also, the Foundation has published a report in 2009, called 'Moving on up', which raises awareness obout the positive benefits that exercise can have on mental health.

Citizens Advice Bureau

www.citizensadvice.org.uk

The Citizens Advice service helps people resolve their legal, money and other problems by providing free, independent and confidential advice, and by influencing policymakers.

ChildLine

www.childline.org.uk

ChildLine is a counselling service for children and young people. Support, advice and help for children up to the age of 18 in the UK, provided by The NSPCC.

FPA

(Family Planning Association), The Sexual Health Charity

www.fpa.org.uk

The FPA provides straightforward information, advice and support to all people across the UK on all aspects of sexual health, sex and relationships.

Department of Work & Pensions/ The Pension Service

www.dwp.gov.uk

For state pension forecasts and information on your state pension.

Her Majesty's Court Service

www.hmcs.gov.uk

For *Form E* financial declaration forms / copies to help with financial budgeting.

The Terence Higgins Trust

www.tht.org.uk

Terrence Higgins Trust is the leading and largest HIV and sexual health charity, established in 1982, in the UK.

Resolution

www.resolution.org.uk

Resolution's 5,500 members are family lawyers committed to the constructive resolution of family disputes.

Nagged, Tagged and Bagged...

About the author

Having worked in the financial services industry for a quarter of a century, and qualified to a high level within UK retail financial services, Keith set up Churchouse Financial Planning Limited with Esther Dadswell in 2004.

A chartered financial planning company in Guildford, Surrey, the company offers independent bespoke advice to clients and enquirers. This ranges from pensions and retirement planning, including tax planning, through to investments, wealth management, business and health and life insurance protection planning. The company is authorised and regulated by the Financial Services Authority.

Keith also completed a BA (Hons) degree in Financial Services in 2007 with Napier University and became a Fellow of the Personal Finance Society in December 2007. In 2008, using Standards International, he was the fourth person in the UK to achieve ISO 22222 Certified Financial Planner status, the British Standard for Personal Financial Planners.

Pensions in divorce have become one of Keith's specialisms. Divorced twice himself, he has some personal knowledge and experience of the overall process. In addition he is a Resolution-accredited Financial Neutral for the divorce process. He has detailed his experiences and learning on the subject of divorce in his second book, *Journey of Divorce, Addicted to Wedding Cake.*

Keith detailed his 25 years' experience in retail financial services in his first book, *Sign Here, Here and Here! . . . Journey of a Financial Adviser.*

Churchouse Financial Planning Limited was Highly Commended at the Gold Standards Awards in both 2007 and 2008.

Keith has made regular expert comment in the local and national press and has frequently been interviewed on the radio over the last six years.

He has an active social media presence and can be found on Linkedin.com and Twitter as @onlinefinancial.

In addition, he tries to have a life outside work, and enjoys writing books, art, keeping fit by cycling and scuba diving.

Bulk Order Form

Nagged, Tagged and Bagged, Divorce Recovery
ISBN 978-0-9564325-4-4

If you would like to place a bulk order (minimum 10 books) for this book you can enjoy a direct discount of 25% per book (plus postage and packaging)

Item	Each	Quantity	Amount
Nagged, Tagged and Bagged, Divorce Recovery. . . (Discounted Rate from £9.99)	£7.49		
Postage (per 10 paperbacks books)			**£15.00***
	Total	£	

Please make cheque and payments payable to:
Churchouse Consultants LLP

Your details:

Name :	
Address :	
Postcode :	
Contact Number/Email :	

Post your order to:
Hadleigh House, 232 High Street, Guildford, Surrey, GU1 3JF

Our contact details for further information:

Tel: *01483 578800*   Fax: 01483 578864
Email: *info@churchouse.com*
www.naggedtaggedandbagged.co.uk

* Price correct at going to press. Postage costs may vary.

Churchouse Consultants LLP
Hadleigh House,
232 High Street,
Guildford,
Surrey,
GU1 3JF

Lightning Source UK Ltd.
Milton Keynes UK
08 March 2011

168868UK00001B/2/P

9 780956 432544